DRIVEN

Hip-Hop, Fast Cars, Basketball and Brain Surgery

The inspirational story
of **Dr. Jason Cormier**
with Mike Harris

DRIVEN
Hip-Hop, Fast Cars, Basketball and Brain Surgery
The inspirational story of Dr. Jason Cormier with Mike Harris

Printed in the United States of America
First Printing: 2022

Cover design by Kenni DeNile
Interior book design by Maureen Cutajar

This book may be purchased in bulk for educational, business, fund-raising or promotional purchases. For information, please contact the publisher at Connectome Entertainment, LLC, P.O. Box 82039, Lafayette, LA 70598, or connectome.publishing@gmail.com

ISBN Ebook: 978-0-578-28256-5
ISBN Print: 978-0-578-28255-8

FOREWORD

Dr. Shaquille O'Neal
Basketball superstar, actor, recording artist and entrepreneur

WHAT'S UP DOC?! Jason Cormier is one guy who could say 'I know I got skillz' on a basketball court, on a racetrack, behind the turntables and in the operating room. He *could* say it, but he doesn't. His life says it for him. He will inspire you to reach your dreams too.

Basketball great Dr. Shaquille O'Neal (left) with retired LSU head coach Dale Brown. (Photo credit: ESPN)

FOREWORD

Dale Brown
Head Coach, LSU Tigers, 1972 – 1997

IF I COULD DESCRIBE Doctor Jason Cormier in one word only, it would be Sophrosyne. It is an ancient Greek concept of an idea of excellence of character and soundness of mind, which combined in one well balanced individual leads to other qualities, such as temperance, moderation, decorum, and self-control.

He is truly a breath of fresh air and I applaud him for his magnificent achievements. He fully understood that life has no remote control and you have to get up and change it yourself. Never did he have an excuse because he was wise enough to understand that excuses are like belly buttons; everybody has one. He has vividly proven that the person who really wants to do something finds a way, while the others find excuses.

CONTENTS

PROLOGUE

It was Mother's Day...

"OH MY GOD!"

Dr. Jason Cormier stopped in his tracks as he entered the Emergency Room and saw the monitor hooked up to the patient.

The call had come from the E.R while he was in surgery at Our Lady of Lourdes Hospital in Lafayette, Louisiana.

"We have a lady here who was in a very severe car accident with one of her sons, her husband and her sister," said the E.R. doctor. "Can you come take a look? It's pretty bad."

"Okay, I'm operating right now," replied Dr. Cormier, "But I'll come over as soon as I'm through here."

About twenty minutes later, he walked into the Emergency Room department. "I was literally ten or fifteen yards away from the monitor and I could see the scan from across the room; it was that dramatic," he recalls. "I said, 'Oh, my God!' before I could stop myself."

As he said those words, the E.R. physician and a young man turned and looked at him. "I thought, 'Oh, this is a little awkward,' as I hadn't realized that it was her other son looking at the images."

When he studied the scan close up, he knew it was as bad – or worse – than he had first thought. "I remember thinking that I wasn't even sure why they consulted me, because this blood clot is so big, there's no way this lady is alive. Apparently, the Radiologist called and told the E.R. physician the same thing: there's no way this lady's alive, it's a terminal injury."

1

The mood in the E.R. was somber. Dr. Cormier looked at the wall calendar and remembered that today was Mother's Day. He thought of his own mother and what he would want someone to do if it had happened to her. He looked at the frightened face of the patient's son and realized her other son had been badly injured in the car wreck too.

He took a deep breath and said, "You know, it's Mother's Day. If there's any sort of movement, motion, anything on her examination, I'm going to take her to the operating room."

Even as he made that decision, he knew he would probably be faulted for it. "A lot of people would say, 'No, don't do that. She doesn't have a good exam, it's a terminal injury, don't do it.'" But Jason Cormier isn't like 'a lot of people'. He accepted the challenge. "Take her to the O.R.," he said.

"I decided to take her to the Operating Room and it was a really sizable blood clot on the right side," he now recalls. "I took the clot out and she survived the operation and she went to ICU following."

He turned his attention to the other members of the family who had been injured in the wreck.

"I went to the other hospital, Lafayette General Medical Center, which was on the other side of the city. I had to see her sister, who had a cervical fracture, and her son who had a really bad lower back fracture. I took him to the Operating Room and had to place instrumentation in his back and fuse him."

He then immediately returned to Our Lady of Lourdes Hospital to see his first patient. "She wasn't moving, her examination hadn't changed," he noted. "Her pupillary function was very dusky which is not a good sign at all. I said, 'Well, let's get another CT scan to make sure the blood clot didn't come back, or there's something else.'"

They ran another CT scan of her brain and it turned out there was another clot on the other side.

"Apparently when I removed one clot, the mass effect pulled the other one or it became more obvious or it took some time to develop," he said. "I took her back to the O.R. emergently the same day and it turned out she had a very severe sagittal sinus injury that is almost a terminal injury. People just do not survive that. It had created something called an epidural hematoma. The first clot was a subdural, a very large subdural hematoma, but this one was an epidural. That surgery lasted an hour-and-a-half to two hours which is extensive but I had to repair the sagittal sinus that was injured in three spots."

After the second surgery, she was taken to the ICU. Dr. Cormier met with her husband there and decided to be completely transparent with him. He recalls the difficult conversation: "We sat down and I said, 'Look, this is really bad. We swung for the fence, but this does not look good. We're going to keep pushing ahead, but if she doesn't really make a turnaround in the next couple of days, it's going to be up to you guys.' He was really appreciative for all the hard work but said, 'No, she wouldn't want to live this way.'"

Dr. Cormier wasn't ready to give up yet. Three days later, he noted that her pupillary function started to improve. "It's not a huge milestone but it's a milestone nonetheless," he said. "Then she kind of started moving her extremities spontaneously. Again, not huge, but it was something. At that point, we decided, okay let's convert her intubated status to a trach – a tracheostomy and PEG tube – and eventually we obtained a CT with an angiogram so we could look at the blood vessels in the brain. And it really didn't look bad. It was relatively normal, actually. The clots were completely gone. There was the stigmata where I had entered the skull but it didn't look bad. I said, 'I don't know how far we're going to get, but her brain doesn't look that bad.'"

Eventually, she was accepted into a rehab facility and still on a mechanical ventilator. The expectation was that this was another patient that would stay on a ventilator and that's how she would live out her last days.

But that's not how this story ends, as we shall see later. And we'll find out why, every year, Mother's Day is still so important to Dr. Jason Cormier.

Dr. Jason Cormier

INTRODUCTION

LONG BEFORE HE EVER thought of becoming a doctor, Jason Cormier was just a kid growing up in Lafayette, Louisiana, where life can be a challenge.

Lafayette is known as 'the Hub City' because it sits at the center of the crossroads formed by I-49 running north-south and I-10 running east-west. It is home to businesses such as Stullers Inc, who sit at the pinnacle of Jewelry settings worldwide, Baker Hughes and Halliburton that service the oil and gas industries and the local economy can depend on the unpredictable volatility of those industries.

Additionally, Mother Nature frequently pounds southern Louisiana with more than its fair share of storms and hurricanes. Sometimes, Life seems to pile challenge on top of challenge.

On paper, the prospects would not look favorable for a young African American, born in Lafayette, whose father abandoned the family, leaving a young mother to raise him and his three siblings on a teacher's pay.

But this young man defied the odds and refused to settle for what Life laid out for him. He went on to play basketball at LSU and professionally, create and release a string of hip-hop and EDM albums, drive race cars, develop safety programs for NASCAR and other contact sports… and become one of America's most respected neurosurgeons.

That man is Jason Cormier. And yes, he is a brain surgeon. A brain surgeon whose other passions happen to include driving very fast and creating beats.

This is his story: how he has faced and overcome every challenge that Life has put in his path. It's an exciting and inspiring story of success. But perhaps more importantly, it's a guide that shows exactly what it takes for you to succeed at the highest levels of anything you want to achieve.

CHAPTER 1

Growing up in Lafayette

"There was the absence of a role model and so we kind of had to figure things out" – John Cormier

LIFE AS A DOCTOR wasn't something that Jason thought about when he was a kid. His focus was entirely on basketball. He would almost literally eat, sleep and breathe basketball. He remembers falling asleep in bed, still clutching his basketball, picturing himself scoring 3-pointers and burying jumpers on an NBA court. Basketball was his life, his passion, his goal.

"He was my second boy and my third child," said Jason's mother Patricia Cormier, "And he was the biggest baby I had!" Jason's siblings are his older brother John and sister Dolores. His younger brother Jeremiah, known as Jerry, would die tragically at the age of twenty-one.

"Our parents got divorced when we were very young, so our mom was really a single mother," said Jason's brother John. "Our father pretty much split and wasn't there for us, so our mother raised four kids on her own and we had to fend for ourselves which was fine. There was the absence of a role model and so we kind of had to figure things out."

Like his siblings, Jason attended Plantation Elementary. His sister Dolores remembers Jason as a child. "He was quiet and he loved music," she said. "Of all of us, he was the most meditative. He was always thinking. We were a bit louder but he was the quieter one."

*Basketball became Jason's favorite sport but he also played
other sports in his youth, including Little League baseball.*

He was the one who was thinking and observing, said Jason's
mom. "He was watching his older brother and sister get into
trouble but he knew not to do it," she said. "He wouldn't do it."

Dolores agreed with that memory. "My other brother John
and I would always be testing with our mom and Jason would
just watch and not do the things we did, so he rarely got into
trouble because he watched what not to do!"

But Jason certainly wasn't a little angel.

"Now I'm not going to say he never got into trouble because, you
know, he was a child indeed," added Dolores, "but he certainly did

less than my brother and I did. Because we were the first two, we were the older two, and you know we tested the waters!"

On one occasion, Jason had been out with some of his friends and suddenly realized he had missed his curfew, and that was something that he didn't want his mom to know about. Rather than face her wrath – and punishment – Jason slipped off his shoes and silently lifted a window that had been left unlocked. He paused. Everything was silent and dark inside the house. Slowly and quietly, he began to climb over the sill.

Suddenly, the room was flooded with light, and there was mom, steely-eyed, her hand on the light switch. "Hi Jason," she said.

There was a pause. "Hi mom," he said.

"And that was it!" said Dolores. "He was always so calm." Like most kids, John and Dolores would probably have started babbling excuses if they had been the ones caught red-handed, but not Jason.

In retrospect, it was an amusing incident. But Jason and his siblings were subjected to punishment – sometimes severe – from their mother. As an adult, Jason reflected on those punishments and how they affected him mentally and physically, as we shall see later.

Another frequent member of the household was Jason's cousin, Royale Colbert, who is now a district court judge in Louisiana.

"Jason's mom practically raised me," said Royale. I lived with them from the time I was about eight years old until I was thirteen or fourteen. Jason and I grew up more like brothers than first cousins."

These days, Royale said that most people address him as Judge and address Jason as Doctor, but as cousins they know each other on a more intimate basis.

"For instance, I recognize his brilliance, but I know the silly things he did," Royale revealed. "I was there when, in the eighth

The Cormier siblings. (L to R) Back row: Jason, John.
Front row: Jeremiah, Dolores

grade, he decided to take his bicycle apart all the way down to the wheel ball bearings. He couldn't figure out how to get the ball bearings back in so he took a hammer and started hammering them back into place. He ended up going through about six sets of ball bearings. He started doing it on a Saturday. He worked on it from Saturday morning until about one or two o'clock in the morning that Sunday and just left it there for three weeks."

Royale continued the story. "We decided to go ride our bicycles three weeks later when his bike is still in a hundred parts. He walks into his room and he puts the bike back together in twenty minutes because he had figured out how to put it back together but just hadn't done it. He had moved on to something else. We go out and ride our bikes then when he gets home, he takes the bike apart again because he wanted to remember how he had put it back together."

It was an early sign of Jason's attention to detail and his fascination with how things work.

CHAPTER 2

The tale of the snake

"He'd told us he'd got bitten by a snake so we'd panicked."
– Dolores Cormier-Zenon

AS OLDER SIBLINGS always do, John and Dolores tended to 'pull rank' on Jason, getting him to do things for them. Quite often, they would send Jason along the road to the corner store to get them some gum or candy. Their mom had some pretty strict rules about what they could and couldn't do while she was at work, out of the house. One of those rules: No going to the store.

Dolores remembers the Saturday afternoon that was the last time it happened:

"Our mother was at a meeting or something and we were at home. So John and I said to Jason, 'Hey, we need to send you to the store.' The corner store near our house. We get all our nickels together and send him to the store with a little list. So off he went to the store and we thought it's taking him a long time to get back. But he finally came back with all of the things."

John and Dolores asked him why it took him so long, because the store was close by. "Oh," Jason told them, "I got bit by a snake."

"Well, John and I, we're kids and we are freaking out," said Dolores. "And we're like, Oh my gosh! We're going through books, trying to find out what type of snake it was and what did it look like. We're so panicked and he points to something and we, like, research it and say, 'I think it's poisonous!' But we're not sure. So then we decide to call an ambulance to get him to Lafayette General, to the Emergency Room."

Right about then, their mom, Patricia, gets home. A science teacher, she was taking continuing education classes on the weekends.

"I remember that time," said Patricia. "I had a class at the local university here. I was going to school that day, on Saturday. When I came back home, Jason said he'd been bitten by a snake so of course I was nervous about that and rushed him to the hospital emergency room. We stayed there until the doctor came and looked at him, at different parts of his arm and his hands but they didn't see any marks of the bite on his skin.

"So I brought him back home and he was okay. I said, 'Jason where were you when you got bitten? And how did it bite you?' He said he reached into the mailbox to get some mail and that's when the snake bit him. I said, 'Are you saying the snake crawled all the way to the mailbox and got inside the mailbox and waited for you to put your hand in there?'"

Dolores picks up the story. "Mom is checking him out and she's talking to him and he's telling her the story. Well, you know how your parents can pick up on the story you're telling is not true. So then mom says, 'You weren't bitten by no snake!'"

Jason's story was convincing, but not quite convincing enough to fool a mother!

"He'd told us he'd got bitten by a snake so we'd panicked," said Dolores thinking back to that strange day. "I think Jason was probably tired of us sending him to the store and getting things for us because we wouldn't go and we'd send him on the errands. That was the end of that errand. He never ran another errand for us after that. But we couldn't tell our mom that we'd sent him to the store because then we'd all be in trouble."

In something of an understatement, Dolores summed it up this way: "Jason was very creative."

CHAPTER 3

Black and poor among the white and wealthy

> *"It put a lot of grit in us, the drive and determination and the will to just not have to go through that again." –* John Cormier

IT WAS AT HIGH SCHOOL that Jason's passion for basketball really came into focus. Jason followed his older brother John and sister Dolores to St. Thomas More High School.

It wasn't exactly a private school, said John, "But it was one of the top schools, if not the top school, in Lafayette. And it was different because there weren't that many people of color in the school."

Here they were, the children of a single mother on a school-teacher's salary, going to the school where the wealthiest people sent their kids. "The black kids who went there were pretty wealthy as well," said John, "So we were the poorest kids in school."

John recalled that it was challenging for the family. "We grew up with hand-me-down clothing," said John. "Our mother just wanted us to have the best education."

There were times when the Cormiers got their food in a hand-me-down fashion from other people, too. John remembers when, for instance, other mothers whose children wouldn't eat fish would give it to their mom and she'd cook it for her kids.

"We had to ration our food so we learned how to make do with less," said John. "It put a lot of grit in us, the drive and determination and the will to just not have to go through that again. And so yeah, I mean it was interesting. Like whether it was academics or athletics, it was just a drive to never have to have that experience again. And our mother did the best she could but as a single mother – and school teachers, they don't make much – going to that kind of school, it just puts a lot of pressure, I think, on a kid, particularly as everyone knows that you're not the kids there that have got the most money."

Like his brother John, Jason couldn't help but feel the financial differential between himself and most of his classmates.

"First of all, you want to belong," Jason points out. "You want to be an equal. You don't want to be a kid that's part of the 'don't-haves' so to speak."

Jason thought back to ways that financial disparity became obvious. For example, it was the different things that the wealthier kids would do. "Like, kids would show up with go-karts, they'd show up on motorcycles, they'd show up in big trucks," he says. "And those are things that my mother could never afford for us. We were always getting rides or hitching rides with other friends.

"Our house, we had a relatively very small house with four kids and a single mother who was a teacher. And so when we'd go to the houses of one of our friends and here it is, I'm coming from my house that might have been maybe 1,100 square feet of living area to a house that's about 7,000 square feet. It's like, 'Wow this is a castle,' you know. And it's one thing after another. These kids have all these different things. We're having to wear some of our uniforms more frequently than they would. It was just a different life."

There's no doubt that it was a challenge to be black and poor in a school where the kids are mainly white and wealthy.

Jason's high school senior photo.

"I mean, we were poor. We weren't dirt poor but we didn't have things like they did," Jason points out. "We didn't have the same shoes, the same pens. It was difficult just trying to belong, not only from a socio-economic standpoint but also from a cultural standpoint as well. I mean, you'd look around and there were only a few Blacks throughout the entire high school, so we were recruited to play sports and that kind of stuff and that was great."

As a general rule, Jason recalls, the differences he experienced were more monetary than racial.

"We were treated well, for the most part, by our other friends and all that, and we were accepted," he says, but adds, "I think in some circles we were more tolerated, I would say. I think the teachers were very fair with us. I didn't feel any sort of discriminatory behavior from the teachers. From that standpoint, we were all treated fairly."

CHAPTER 4

Wrongly accused in the cafeteria

"Our parents went ballistic. They were up at the school the next day and they were fit to be tied. I mean, they just let the principal have it." – Jason Cormier

HOWEVER, ONE PARTICULAR INCIDENT at St. Thomas More High School has remained in Jason's memory. It involved Jason and three of his friends – all African Americans – and a cafeteria worker.

"All the African Americans sat together, at least all the guys did, so this unspoken feeling or need to separate was clear and every now and then, there would be people from other races," he says. "But for the most part at lunch, all the black guys hung together. We were talking about a lot of the same things, a lot of TV shows, whatever, and it was fine. It was whatever it was. But then when it came to sports and the different clubs or whatever, of course the groups were more mixed and it felt natural, we were all brothers."

Jason explains the background. "Four of us were in line at the cafeteria," he recalls, "It was me, Troy Taylor, Brien Syrie and Larry Moore. We had all attempted to carve different designs or symbols into each other's hair. I got Troy to carve a Mercedes logo into my hair, or at least that's what it was meant to be. It didn't really look too authentic, I guess, because we didn't really know what we were doing, nonetheless I thought I was cool!"

As they were in line, the cafeteria lady claimed she had been insulted by one of them. "She heard someone say something like, 'Pick that up,'" says Jason, "Or something that she thought was rude or something offensive, apparently. She complained to the principal and she said it was 'one of those boys that has a scar on his head.'"

It didn't take long for the incident to escalate.

"The four of us all got hauled off to the principal's office," says Jason. The principal told them that the cafeteria lady had reported them and complained that one of them had been rude. "The principal told us, 'Look, you know you guys are going to have to apologize to this lady for saying what you said.' We're all like, 'Well, what did we say? We didn't say anything.' And he said, 'Well, the lady said that somebody with a scar on his head or who had some sort of emblem said something to her.' And we're looking at each other like, 'Okay, what is she talking about?' There was one guy who had, I forget exactly, but it was some kind of symbol in his hair. Another guy had just kind of a couple of hash marks in his hair. And we're like, 'Well, but we didn't say anything.'"

All four of the guys were shocked by the complaint but eventually realized that the principal was adamant. To resolve the situation, he told them to apologize to the cafeteria lady and present her with a rose.

"We're like, okay, whatever," says Jason. "It's just a rose or something we'll have to give her. We'll just bring it to school tomorrow. So we went home and we all told our parents."

However, when Jason's mother and the other guys' parents heard what the principal had ordered them to do, they were not happy, to say the least.

"Our parents went ballistic," says Jason. "They got on the phone with each other and they were up at the school the next day and they were fit to be tied. I mean, they just let the principal have it. And, you know, after it was all said and done, there were no roses given to this lady and no apologies. Our parents just said, 'No way.'"

The four students involved were all African-American and the parents believed they had been singled out and treated unfairly. Race definitely appeared to be a factor.

"Because of that, we actually were looking to transfer out of there," admits Jason. "We were looking at a different school after that happened and then I think Coach Danny Broussard kind of got involved in it as well. He was a big support for us just in terms of keeping us together and keeping us at St. Thomas More. Because we really felt like we had been given a negative shake, so to speak."

CHAPTER 5

The home court advantage

"He was a very focused player and I think the thing about Jason was that he's one of those players that was very unselfish and he made other players better." – Coach Danny Broussard

COACH DANNY BROUSSARD. If there was one man who had a positive effect on Jason's life while he was at St. Thomas More High School, it was his basketball coach, Danny Broussard. He became something of a mentor to Jason.

"I think really his whole purpose was providing a solid foundation in all of us," Jason notes. "He was really, I think, the beginning of what it meant for me to understand what a team was truly all about, how to accept situations beyond your control, and how you stand up for your other teammates. So yeah, like any coach, he has his ways of coaching, but at the same time, I think what he meant to us was he provided a foundation upon which you train and understand fundamentals of basketball and once you get that established, you can go many different places. And so that's probably the biggest thing that I remember from him. Looking back, my opportunities were limited, but in the end it created a deeper passion to move past anyone attempting to hold me back. Don't let anyone define how good you are at something, believe in God and in yourself and go for it."

Danny Broussard is still coaching at St. Thomas More and has been for almost 40 years. It was a job that almost didn't happen.

St. Thomas More High School basketball coach Danny Broussard

"My brother was the head coach for the very first year of Saint Thomas More's existence and I was an assistant," explained Danny. "The next year, we'd already started the school year and my brother got offered a job at the local university which is now the University of Louisiana at Lafayette. We'd already started school and I was 22 years old so they were kind of forced to give me the job." With a laugh, he added, "I mean, who were they going to get?"

Danny has had a remarkable career as a coach. He is the third-winningest coach in Louisiana history with more than one thousand wins and has a good chance to become number one eventually.

Danny remembers the first year that Jason was on the basketball team. The previous year, St. Thomas More won the Louisiana State championship. The year after that win, the team was, if anything, even better. Many of the players from the winning team were coming back, and some fresh talent, including Jason, were eligible to play. They had a great year and almost repeated the championship.

Danny remembers that season vividly. "We went 38 and 2," he said. "We only lost two games and we lost the state championship game to Washington Marion from Lake Charles. We were even nationally ranked. That was Jason's junior year when we were nationally ranked 21st in the country by USA Today. So Jason played for me at a time when we had one of our most talented group of players."

Having such a strong team meant that Danny had a deep pool of talent to draw from. "It was hard for him to crack the starting lineup," Danny frankly admitted. "Not that he wasn't a very good player, as you can tell. I mean, he walked on at LSU and became a scholarship player so that tells you he was talented. It was just at the time he was playing for us, we were probably at our most talented stretch of teams ever. We just had a great, great run right then, when he was there."

Coach Broussard recognized some specific character traits in Jason that were developing during his time on the school's basketball team that would stay with him throughout his life.

"Jason brought real energy to practice," he said. "He was a very focused player and I think the thing about Jason was that he's one of those players that was very unselfish and he made other players better because Jason wasn't one of those kids that was worried about how many points he scored. He was one of those guys that was competitive, he wanted to win and would do whatever it took for our team to be successful and he was a very unselfish player."

It was apparent to Danny that Jason was not one of the louder team members and wasn't one to brag about his achievements. "He was very soft spoken," Danny noted. "I do remember this about him as a basketball player, Jason was very focused. I would say he was very intense on the court but again, very focused. He was a serious player. I'm one of those coaches that likes to have fun at practice. Not to say that he wouldn't have fun and he would crack up and joke, but when it came time to be serious Jason was a very serious basketball player."

Jason's connection to Coach Broussard didn't end when he left high school. "We are good friends today and he continues to be supportive and proud of me for both my internal growth and professional success," says Jason. "He still stays in contact with all of us today. So he's always trying to bring the teams back together and I try to keep up with them."

As Danny noted, Jason wasn't as loud and assertive as many of the other students at the school. "Back then, I wasn't as close to him as he was to some other players because I was an introvert," Jason admits, "But I understood what he was saying, what he gave to us. I credit him with igniting the passion within myself to never lose sight of success and to be there for other people."

For Jason, it was his determination to excel at basketball that made the difficult times worthwhile.

"I was really, really deep into sports," says Jason emphatically, about his life at high school. "I was going to be an NBA basketball player; that was it. I had two siblings ahead of me, my older sister and my older brother. They were pretty good athletes; my sister ran track and my brother played football and track and so basketball made sense to me, but I also played a lot of baseball. My mother kept us in sports so that was really the foundation, at least from an athletics point of view."

Perhaps foreshadowing his later interest in medicine, he adds, "And because she was a biology science teacher, we were kind of immersed in that pretty quickly in life."

CHAPTER 6

Stay out of jail and get an education

"A lot of our drive came from watching our mom work really hard to make the sacrifices so that we had some food on the table." – John Cormier

JOHN CORMIER BELIEVES that their mother's attitude was probably shaped by her own background. "She didn't come from the best environment, but she was just determined," he acknowledged. "In fact, our mom, after my dad left, what she just wanted was for us to not go to jail. She's like, 'Don't go to jail and get an education and you can do whatever you want'. And she'd always say, 'Whatever it is you do, be the best at it; no matter what it is, just be the best at it.' And so for us, a lot of our drive came from watching our mom work really hard to make the sacrifices so that we had some food on the table or something. We were in a situation where we didn't have as much as everyone else, so you work harder because you feel like you should be able to have these things. So we just worked harder. We just bore down diligently to get certain things done so that we could actually survive."

Jason's cousin, Royale Colbert, who lived in the Cormier household for much of his childhood, could see the clash of personalities between Jason and his mother. "I know Jason's life has always been a series of challenges, some good some bad," said Royale. "A lot of the challenges were self-inflicted because it's something he wanted to do that my aunt Patricia, who is a strong personality, might not have agreed with and he had to do it his way. That was the clash between the two of them. My aunt is a strong disciplinarian, she's a strong academician. Her thing was, 'You go to school, you concentrate on school, you make good grades. I don't want to hear anything else.' Jason's attitude was, 'I can go to school, but I can learn other stuff, too.'"

The influence that Jason's mother had on him was apparent to Coach Broussard, both academically and in sports.

"I didn't know exactly the details about his father," Danny said frankly, "But his mother was raising him. She was a teacher at a public school. She was very engaged, very active in the community, and I really loved her as a parent because I found that he had such a great upbringing."

Danny noted that Jason's mother took a close interest in her children's school life as a foundation for their future. "She wanted to see him in an environment that was a good education and a family community type thing in the basketball environment and I really remember that about her," says Danny. "She was a very supportive mother with Jason. As his mom, she was very active, she came to all the games, she was very supportive of me as a coach, and I've always appreciated that about her. She always told me that she was entrusting me with her kid. She knew that I was going to discipline him when needed and encourage him, and that's what I tried to do with him."

There were times when Jason felt that the encouragement was coming almost exclusively from Coach Broussard and his teammates rather than from his mother whose insistence on academic excellence would clash with Jason's sporting ambitions.

Looking back now, Jason thinks that Coach Broussard was probably unaware of just how strict the discipline was that Jason had to deal with at home. Additionally, Jason recalls that his mother often expressed suspicion about the motives of coaches in general, rather than specifically about Coach Broussard.

"My mother would tell us that all coaches do is that they use their players," says Jason. "She would say, 'The coaches don't want to see any good things come from it in terms of academics and academics is the only thing you should focus on. You've got to listen to mom and that's that.'"

Lyle Mouton, like many of Jason's school friends, shared his burning passion for sports. Jason and Lyle have known each other since they were kids.

"Jason's family and my family were friends before we were born," said Lyle. "Both our sets of parents were born and raised in Lafayette as well. We went to primary school together, elementary school, junior high, high school; we were in college together. So we go way back. Our high school actually was a consolidation of three Catholic schools that turned into one high school. We were at the same Catholic elementary and junior high that fed into St. Thomas More High School."

Lyle excelled at both basketball and baseball. After high school, like Jason, he went to LSU where he played as a guard before focusing solely on baseball, leading the LSU Tigers to three straight College World Series tournaments and two back-to-back SEC championships. After LSU, Lyle moved on to professional baseball as an outfielder, playing for the Chicago White Sox, Baltimore Orioles, Milwaukee Brewers and Florida Marlins. He also played in Japan for the Yakult Swallows.

Jason's cousin, Royale Colbert, saw Jason's talent on a baseball field too. "He never played football much, but mainly basketball and baseball with basketball being his passion and baseball being his natural talent. Again, this is my personal experience and everybody in the family was a college athlete. Jason probably could have been a pro baseball player, but his passion was towards basketball. But if he was ever honest with himself or asked me to be honest with him, having observed and watched him and growing up with him, he was five times the baseball player than he was a basketball player, and he was a great basketball player. He played college basketball, he worked hard at it, but he was a natural baseball player. It came to him naturally. He could do what he wanted with a baseball. If he wanted to hit it right, he could hit it right. If he wanted to hit it left, he could hit it left. He was a natural baseball player, but he preferred to play basketball. I love him like a brother, but my honesty toward him would be, 'You should have been a professional baseball player because you would have done it easily.'"

CHAPTER 7

Hard work beats raw talent

"If you give up early you don't find your 'aha' moment or you don't know when your talent in whatever you're doing becomes fruitful." – Lyle Mouton

LYLE MADE A SIGNIFICANT point about Jason's personality. "From a sporting standpoint, Jason wasn't always the best, but he had the stick-to-itiveness to work at his craft, especially when we got to high school," Lyle noted. "We had a very strong, very dominant, very talented high school team, and Jason wasn't always, you know, front line playing. He probably didn't start or play a lot into his senior year, but that didn't stop him from working on his craft and continuing to want to be part of the tradition."

It was a characteristic that would stay with Jason beyond high school. "It even led into college," said Lyle, "where his love of the game, his working on his craft, not getting into school on any kind of basketball scholarship, but going out as a walk-on and making the team."

Stick-to-itiveness is a word that comes up frequently when friends and colleagues talk about Jason Cormier; either stick-to-itiveness or a similar phrase that describes Jason's dedication to complete – and excel at – any project he undertakes. It's a character trait that he shares with his siblings and one that bloomed and developed while playing basketball at St. Thomas More High School.

Jason's long-time friend and team-mate Lyle Mouton put it this way: "If you give up early you don't find your 'aha' moment or you don't know when your talent in whatever you're doing becomes fruitful. You may not have stuck with it long enough to let it grow and mature and then blossom because you didn't get the success you wanted early. You gave up on it. Jason didn't do that."

Another long-time friend and teammate Troy Taylor said, "Jason was one of the most athletic guys on the team and while his opportunities were limited in high school sports, that never stopped him from achieving his dream! Despite the odds, he persevered and never gave up!"

Troy has gone on to become owner of the fastest growing Coca-Cola distributorship in the United States and through this and many other entrepreneurial ventures is now a self made billionaire. "We are cut from the same thread and we pray to the same God, so to surrender or give up is just not our blood," said Troy.

Another school friend, James Ambroise, formed a similar impression of Jason. "He always struck me as a hard worker, good sense of humor, definitely open to trying new things," said James. "He was pretty focused on trying to be the best that he could be."

Although James wasn't on the basketball team – he ran track – he was the team's statistician and got to observe Jason on the court. Like Coach Danny Broussard, James saw Jason as the one with the tenacity to keep on striving while competing for a place on a team full of naturally-gifted players.

"For example, he may not necessarily have been the best player on the basketball team, but he didn't let that stop him from going out and playing with the team and working hard to improve his skills and develop his skills and all of that stuff," said James, echoing the coach's observations. "He's definitely always been a hard worker in that respect and has a good work ethic. I remember that very clearly about him, I think, in all aspects of what he did."

Another friend and high school teammate was Nolan Guidry who remembers Jason as being very self-motivated.

"Jason was very ambitious," Nolan emphasized. "What I remember most about Jason, I think of him as a young man being ambitious. He had dreams and goals of things that he wanted to do, like we all did in high school, but he was very determined."

Nolan said that this was very apparent when it came to basketball. "That was our biggest common thread at the time," he said. "We were on a freshman team, and then when you graduate and become a sophomore, you would try out for either Junior Varsity or you try for the Varsity."

For Nolan, there was something about Jason that he noticed even then.

"What I do remember is that out of all the guys, Jason, at that age, had a self-imposed work ethic that was much more mature than a lot of us. Even though we were all talented, he had a good work ethic. He was always working on his strength, his endurance, to try to give himself an edge or an advantage when trying out for basketball and trying out for the team and even in the classroom."

Nolan added, "He's very intelligent but he always worked hard and he always was focused. He set goals. He did that in basketball which I was very impressed with, and as young men, teens in high school, you don't normally get that way until we're in college or much later. But he was very focused at a young age."

Brien Syrie remembers being in the same class at St Thomas More as Jason and also on the same basketball team. As Brien noted, the students at the school were predominantly white.

"Our class, the one Jason and I were in, we had the most Blacks that graduated in the class," said Brien. "I think we had, like, twelve or thirteen in the class and I don't think STM has had that many ever since."

Brien doesn't recall experiencing any overt racism during their time at high school. But he added, "I'm sure it existed. Now, did the school go out their way to be extra nice to us? That possibly could have happened. But, me personally, I didn't face any one-on-one personal racism if you want to call it that. I don't know if they went out their way to be extra nice or extra careful around us. I'm not sure."

CHAPTER 8

Shooting hoops in the rain

"It would rain and most people would use that as an excuse. But he would practice at night outside in the rain. It was his drive, I think, to be successful." – John Cormier

BRIEN SAID THAT JASON was continually working on improving his basketball skill. "Oh yeah, he was always playing somewhere," he nodded. "We would all always play somewhere, but he would do a lot of individual work. I could see his progress from, say, sophomore year to junior year. You could tell the progress he made in the summertime. He'd been working on something because you could see the progress."

As Brien observed, what made the difference for Jason was that he was not content to rely on the team's regular practice sessions. For him, being good enough was never going to be good enough. He would practice continually, alone or in pick-up games, putting in the hard work to develop skills that came easily for more naturally-gifted players.

If you are going to be the best that you can be, you have to go the extra mile – and then some. It was a discipline, developed in high school, that would be a keystone to his success at every stage of his life.

Jason's older brother John remembers when Jason was trying out for the basketball team. "He was very determined to make the team," said John. "He would practice every day. He would

Jason at basketball team practice, St. Thomas More High School

study then he'd practice at night. It would rain and most people would use that as an excuse. But he would practice at night outside in the rain. It was his drive, I think, to be successful."

Jason became a familiar sight to the Cormiers' neighbors, taking shot after shot at the hoop in the driveway, often late into the dark of night, regardless of the weather.

"That's just one example," said John, adding, "At that time, I knew that whatever he pursued, he would be very successful at it because of his sheer will to succeed."

Brien agreed. "He was definitely going to outwork you, for sure," he acknowledged.

However much Jason might want to practice, it was 'study first, then practice', as John Cormier mentioned.

"Education had to come first in that household," said Brien. "I could see the drive he had. He came from a single-parent household and it always drove him to be successful. His mother saw education as important, so that was a big part of his drive."

In addition to his mother's insistence on the importance of a good education, there was a further incentive. "You had to maintain a certain GPA to play sports," stipulated Brien, "and Jason always played sports. He was always on the team so he never fell short as far as the education requirement to stay on the team. He went far beyond that. His mom put the emphasis on it, because without education, good grades, you wouldn't have been on the basketball team, first of all."

Jason's high school teammate Nolan Guidry echoed those thoughts. "I can definitely understand that," he said. "I think a lot of that comes from his upbringing. His mom was in education. His mom was pretty stern and raised him and his brother and sister to believe that there's nothing that you can't do if you work hard."

Sports were important but were not allowed to supplant the emphasis on attaining an education that would support them throughout their lives after they finished school.

"In our graduating class that Jason and I were in, we had athletes but actually we had the valedictorian in that class too," said Nolan, who is now a Compliance Manager for Allstate Insurance in McKinney, Texas. "So yes, we had great athletes, but we had good students too. I mean, we had a good mix of talent on both sides of the spectrum."

A good coach can build a winning team on the basketball court or the football field. A great coach sees his role as a character-builder that can influence the lives of his team members for decades into the future. Nolan sees the ever-enthusiastic Danny Broussard at St. Thomas More High School as that kind of coach. "He has been that way ever since I set foot in that high school, and he is that same way today," said Nolan. "We still keep in touch. He's a great motivator. He reaches the kids and he reached all of us off the court as well so that we could be not just good basketball players but better men."

Jason Cormier recalls the influence that Coach Danny had on him and his fellow team members. "He really instilled not only teamwork but to do your part," says Jason. "Be fundamentally sound. And that's another one of those things that I did get from him. Put yourself in positions to give yourself the best opportunity to succeed."

CHAPTER 9

Prepared to be 'lucky'

"I don't think I really went to look for those people. I think God put people in my path. I'm a strong believer of that. I just feel that my faith and my belief system and through the good Lord, people are put in my path." – Jason Cormier

BEING PREPARED TO TAKE advantage of opportunities when they present themselves has become a major part of Jason's skill set as we shall see. Almost always, opportunities appear in our lives unexpectedly. When we want something but do nothing to make it happen, it's simply a wish. When we prepare ourselves by acquiring skills and developing the right attitude, it becomes a goal. When a way to achieve that goal suddenly appears, we're ready to seize it and run with it.

Sometimes, successful people are described as being 'lucky,' 'a fluke' or 'getting all the breaks.' But it's surprising how lucky you can get when you have prepared yourself for just this eventuality. You can move forward with confidence in your capabilities and boldly grasp the opportunity where others would simply let it slip away like sand running between their fingers. Perhaps race car driver Bobby Uncer phrased it perfectly: "Success is where preparation and opportunity meet." That attitude has certainly worked for Uncer, part of the remarkable Uncer auto racing family who, between them, have won the Indy 500 a record nine times.

Jason has repeatedly found himself in front of people who have made a difference in his life. This has been true with his love of basketball, his interest in music, his fascination with auto racing, his remarkable career in medicine and surgery. In each case, those people recognized his capability and – equally important – his passion to succeed.

"I don't think I really went to look for those people," Jason says with disarming modesty. "I say I think God put people in my path. I'm a strong believer of that. I was an altar boy through elementary and high school at the local church, and I just feel that my faith and my belief system and through the good Lord, people are put in my path. Things happen that create this path. And now with all these things coming together, who would have thought a lot of things would be so well merged together and now all travel in the same direction. With Coach Brown, I didn't necessarily know that I would go to LSU or even med school or through St. Thomas More."

Early in his life, Jason developed the self-discipline to make success happen. "I can tell you, when I first started playing basketball," he says, "It was one of those things where I would sleep with a basketball because I saw this thing about Mike Tyson when he was first coming up and he said, 'I do different things, I'll run in the rain because I know the other guys aren't doing it.' And so even at the age of like ten, eleven years old, I would go out in the rain and I would shoot basketball because I figured, well, the other guy wasn't doing it so maybe I can get an edge."

Jason is candid about the thoughts that were motivating him as he continued to practice while the Louisiana rain soaked him to the skin. "I used to imagine that the lightning were the cameramen snapping pictures of me and the thunder was like people trying to make me miss. So then I would do other things, like just dribble in the rain with my left hand all the way to church or shoot in the rain." He smiles at the memory. "People that passed by our driveway thought I was nuts, I'm sure." With his focus on the ball and the net, Jason didn't even notice them.

"I think part of the driving force was just trying to succeed, to overcome difficulty, of which there were a number in my life," he says, in something of an understatement. "My next-door neighbor, Barry Olivier, was actually playing for St. Thomas More, and he and my older brother used to beat the heck out of me at basketball and I was a sore loser. At the time, I thought Barry was the best player in the world. I mean, he was my albatross. He was the one I just had to get that one win off. If I could beat him, I could beat anybody.

"Then finally I started growing and my height started catching up with my talent, and so I started beating him convincingly. And that's when it was just my drive, it was my passion; my goal was to beat him and now it was that one hurdle and finally I beat him and then I kind of just moved up the ladder."

Lyle Mouton was a year ahead of Jason when he got to St. Thomas More High School. As with being able to beat his next-door neighbor, beating Lyle became Jason's next hurdle.

"I was following Lyle who played basketball and was a superstar at St. Thomas More and we got to LSU, and Lyle was great; he was a multi-sports athlete, very athletic, very gifted in many sports. And he was another one. I was like, 'If I can beat him one-on-one, man!' And that's it, he was another one. It took me several tries until one time I finally did it. So it's just one of those things. I may not beat you the first time. It may take a hundred games but one of those games I'm going to win."

CHAPTER 10

Mommie Dearest?

"You tell me I can't do this, I'm gonna do it big time."
– Jason Cormier

HAVING A STRONG-WILLED, assertive mother can be a double-edged sword. There's no doubt that Patricia Cormier took an intense interest in the lives of her children, particularly with regard to their education. As a single mother, she took on the role of both mother and father, often feeling compelled to act in situations – such as discipline and dealing with coaches – that would traditionally be handled by a father.

However, there are times when that kind of attention can feel like interference, even manipulation, to a young man like Jason with a mind of his own.

"I mean, my mother was this 'hard knocks' woman, a female that would not let any male really tell her anything," says Jason now. "She could never be wrong. And some ways she handled things, I felt, were manipulative because we would get pulled out of sports, pulled out of certain things and then reinserted with expectations that we would start the next basketball game but that's not really fair to the other players or the coaches. And because of that she would say, 'Well fine, you didn't play or you didn't start so I'm just gonna take you off the team.'"

Jason says that his mother would object if she thought practice was going on too long, cutting into time when he and the other kids should be studying. "My mother had never really competed in any college sport or any competitive sport in high school, but you would think that she was a high school coach in the way that she approached these situations, and it became embarrassing," he recalls. "I would have to face my coach, but he's dealing with my mother who was really not as nice and approachable as some of the other parents of the kids I was playing with."

It was humiliating for Jason to be caught in the middle of these situations. "Quite frankly, there were so many people that did not want to deal with my mother in situations like this because she appeared so overbearing," he notes. "Her attitude was, 'I'm going to have the last word or else I'm going to be taking my son out of the program'. It was like a game of chess and we were the pawns."

It is evident that Jason felt a lot of frustration at the control that his mother exerted over every aspect of his life. He developed a steely attitude to show the world – including his mother – that he had what it takes to be a winner.

"She would say I wouldn't finish something," he contends. "And, really, part of what I did was to prove her wrong. Yeah, I'm going to be good at basketball, I am going to be good in school and now here I am."

Patricia Cormier confirmed the friction that existed between them. "I said, 'I'm not sending you to school to play basketball, you're there to get an education'," she recalled. "I was very strict on all of them. I thought my kids would grow up hating me. They used to call me, like that movie, *Mommie Dearest*," a biographical film about movie star Joan Crawford from the point of view of her adopted daughter.

"Jason was very upset with me. For several years, he hardly spoke to me," she said. "Eventually he decided that he was ready to converse more often."

Looking back, Jason can see the possible origin of his mother's attitude. "I guess maybe that comes from a cultural thing too, from her background, the way she was brought up," he allows.

"People deal with stress in different ways and I think she reacted and acted out of what she probably knew and that was from her own upbringing because she had been abused as well although I don't know to what extent; my sister knows more about that than I do.

"My mother didn't do drugs she didn't drink, she would hardly ever curse," he notes. "I might have heard my mother curse maybe a dozen times, but it wasn't like she had this 'playground mouth' where she cursed all the time. So yes, I mean the stress and the way she reacted to it and being a single mother and having to push education, and my father wasn't really doing his part so that was stressful with having to go back and forth, from an authority standpoint, to get him to pay child support and all that."

Jason recognizes that all played a part but adds, "I just don't know how violence became a part of that as a resolution. I'm sure she's sorry for some of those things, or I would hope so, but yeah, that's kind of what we had to go through."

Jason was able to immerse himself in what he felt was a more positive and encouraging environment outside the home.

"My relationships with my friends," he recalls, "I guess the group of friends I had, we encouraged and supported each other in a positive way. I had outlets, I had basketball, I had music and I had all that, I guess, to try to buffer the system if you will, to stay happy and stay focused on other things I wanted to do."

Jason recalls that, at the time, he was just trying to get through it like his brother and sister before him.

"We were just trying to survive," he says, "Eating on Sunday and maybe we wouldn't eat again until Wednesday. My mother was rationing food. We were literally trying to survive, many times having to cook for ourselves. There were instances where she wasn't home. Now, I don't want to say that the house was void of love. There were some times when she did say, 'I love you,' but it was so confusing and such an awkward way to live because you didn't know when your head was going to get smacked, when you were going to get whipped or when you're going to get awakened with ice out of a deep sleep."

Jason acknowledges that there were probably many other kids that had it worse than he did, but he adds, "Many times it felt like I was a pawn and I had to fight through a lot of the negativity. That created not only pain from emotional abuse but also physical abuse."

There were times, Jason says, that his mother would tell them things like, "I wish you guys were never born," or "You make me want to throw up," or "You remind me of your dad whom I loathe."

That was the emotional aspect, but from the physical standpoint, he recalls some traumatic occasions from his childhood. "My mother would make us sleep outside, my mother would wake us up with ice while we were sleeping in the morning before school, she would whip us with sticks, she would whip us with these toy race tracks, she would whip us with brooms and she would slap our ears. And sometimes she would do this in public so that was humiliating as well as painful."

Thinking back now, he says, "That makes you more introverted and makes you stay to yourself out of embarrassment. It makes you not want to engage in certain things because of how people are going to look at you. Maybe you are giving your all but your all might not be good enough for anyone because it wasn't good enough for mom because she didn't say 'I'm proud of you' all that much."

It became part of Jason's motivation on his path to success. "I just knew I didn't want to have the life that I was living as a sort of permanence going forward in the future," he says.

Later in life, Jason happened to meet a psychiatrist socially and they got into conversation about his achievements. "I think the crescendo hit me when I spoke to this psychiatrist," he recalls, "and she told me, 'I think that you succeed to spite the people that hurt you.' And that was part of it. Yeah. You tell me I can't do this, I'm gonna do it big time. Honestly, I didn't think anything of it though; I was just talking because I didn't really believe in them [psychiatrists] at the time."

Jason acknowledges that his mother has played a role in the success he has achieved in life, even if much of it was to prove her wrong. How would things have been different if his relationship with his mother had been more positive? "I think it sounds horrible," he admits, "But I would have accomplished a lot less, yet I would have appreciated what I have accomplished a lot more."

Jason's cousin, Royale Colbert, could see the clash of personalities between Jason and his mother.

"My Aunt Patricia is the first college graduate in our family," Royale noted. "I would say, except for her getting married at an early age to the wrong person, my aunt would probably be a doctor herself. But my aunt is also educationally obsessed. She loves being a teacher and she loves being in the realm of academics.

"Like most African-American mothers, my Aunt Pat still feels, 'I'm your mama. I still know better than you.' So that's the conflict. I understand his frustration, but I mean, she's raised some great children. All of her children are extremely successful."

As his cousin, Royale has a frank observation: "So yes, Jason, while you're a neurosurgeon and you're smarter than the average person, your mama did a damn good job. I mean, Dolores has a PhD, John graduated from Wharton School of Business. Hell, I'm going to give her credit for me, too. I made Major in the United States Army and now I'm a district court judge. My aunt did a good job and now she loves telling us, 'I did a good job.' That's their conflict. She doesn't ever want to be told she's wrong. But neither does he."

Royale recalled disagreements that resulted in Jason and his mother not speaking for months at a time. "Then my aunt got sick and had to go into the hospital and before anybody knew what's happening, Jason was at her bedside. So it's a revolving door."

"Royale came into our household and he was our cousin and it was great and all that," says Jason. "But he was also treated differently to the way we were treated. So while we may have succeeded, it was more so because at the time I'm looking up to my brother and he was really a superstar in high school, or to my sister who was helping to care for us. It was more of a familial support group, if you will. It wasn't because Mom constantly promoted us to become so successful, outside of homework, which was important, and she made education her primary focus."

Jason's mother was a teacher at a public high school at the time. "She would bring some of these kids into our home to live with us for like a year at a time," says Jason. "These kids were impoverished and did not grow up in the best surroundings. Some of them were really hardened by the system and much older than we were, in the same grade. They were nice to us, for sure, and they had a room and an area to sleep. It was surprising, after we'd finally get to know what their history was, I couldn't believe it. I was like, 'these guys had done some really horrible things, and they had horrible things happen to them.' They too were survivors. She brought them into our house, and at times it seemed that she cared for them more than she cared for us. We would get punished as usual, yet they did not seem to fall under the same rules."

Thinking back to the time that his mom caught him sneaking back into the house through a window, he notes, "They were allowed to stay out late at night. She hardly ever enforced that with them, but she certainly enforced it with us. In the end this turned out to be a good thing for many reasons. But there was no explanation. It was just, 'You're not going to do it. I'm your mom.' You couldn't fight it or you were going to get slapped or something."

He says that some of those kids could see the difference in the way they were treated. "Sometimes they would say things like, 'She's more of a mom to me than she is to you. She treats me nicer.' When we'd bring that back to her, sometimes we'd get hit and sometimes we were told, 'Well, that's not for you guys to understand. And you can't ask questions because I'm Mom.' That was one of her favorite things to say. 'You can't ask questions.'"

Jason and his siblings could feel the difference, emotionally and physically. "We didn't have half an inch to mess up," he says bluntly. "There was punishment, there was a whipping, a beating, and so on. Really it was a couple of things. She was like, 'I'm going to bring these kids in, I'm going to turn their lives around and make them better. But I'm still going to stay the course with my own kids.'"

Looking back, he says, "When you're that young, you start thinking, 'Well, she's finding kids that are better than her own kids. Or she wants to believe that she can raise them better and that's where her preference now lies.'"

He has a distressing revelation about that aspect of his childhood.

"There were times when I was being beaten when I wished God would take me now because nothing could be worse than this," he says. "I was pleading, 'God, please take me. Life after this has got to be better than this. I don't want to live through another beating.' You're going to school with bruises, you're getting what she called getting your ears boxed. You're literally seeing stars and what I know now were concussions, getting smacked on both ears like it was no big deal."

The punishments seemed out of proportion to whatever it was that he had apparently said or done. "I don't feel like we were deserving," he says, "And certainly I know there were others that had it so much worse than we did. I mean, we did not get shot or stabbed."

In a moment of reflection, he adds, "I feel like my mother – at least at times – felt that she was doing the best that she could."

Jason believes that brutality is unjustified when you're trying to raise a child. "Despite all of it, I still love my mother," he says, "And I am thankful both to her and to God for the strength and perseverance I found to push through the most difficult times that led to my faith, hope, success, happiness, and now true love."

Based on his own experience, Jason has some important thoughts to share with parents. "I think that all mothers should remember that the things you tell your kids, the things you do to your kids, can go a long way. You are the first teacher of that child, so you are essentially the first builder of the next generation, the builder of the next world, and kids listen. Children are going to listen to everything you tell us, good, bad or ugly."

CHAPTER 11

Finding hip-hop, making music

"I wanted to be a DJ so I even had a piece of wood and I stenciled out 'Cut Master Jay.' That was the name I gave myself." – Jason Cormier

IF BASKETBALL WAS THE main focus – even obsession – for young Jason, music wasn't far behind. He loved music, particularly R&B and hip-hop. As often happens, Jason was drawn into a friendship with others who shared his musical interests.

"We actually met when we were about seven or eight years old," said Carl Martin, who – as Carl 'Groove' Martin – went on to form the R&B group Shai. "Actually, Jason was my first collaborator, technically. We started a little hip-hop duo when we were about twelve."

Just as Jason and Carl reached the age where music becomes a part of any kid's life, the music itself was beginning to change. Hip-hop and rap music had been around since the 1970s, growing from a musical subculture that began in neighborhoods in the Bronx in New York City. Initially, it was heard only at block parties, partly evolving from Jamaican 'toasting' where a DJ would rap – or 'toast' – ad-libbed lyrics over instrumental tracks played on record turntables. Not long after that, record labels discovered some of the early rappers and the popularity of hip-hop music spread nationwide, particularly among African-American teens. Early rap stars such as Grandmaster Flash and Kurtis Blow recorded hits that crossed over to mainstream pop. By the mid 1980s, new stars, including Run D.M.C. and LL Cool J were emerging, and this music, the 'new school' hip-hop was what really spoke to Jason.

It was a hip-hop culture; not only the music itself but an entire lifestyle that encompasses attitudes, clothing, cars and breakdancing. It was a culture that attracted Jason and his friends such as Carl Martin and Marcus Brown.

Long before hip hop even existed, music had been in the Cormier home since Jason was an infant and it's the sound of a piano that forms his earliest musical memory.

"When we were young, I think I must have been five or six years old, my mother played the piano and she'd play the piano for this small church that was on the outskirts of Lafayette," Jason recalls. "We used to go there and sing with her and it was kind of a mandatory thing."

Jason's mother encouraged her children to take piano lessons. His sister Dolores began to play the piano, but as Jason says, "I didn't do quite so well because at that point in time, I was chasing basketball, but it was mandatory that we go in and sing with her at those Sunday services. My mother used to play the piano at home a lot too, I guess to just practice different songs before it was time to play in church."

The years passed and a whole young generation discovered hip-hop, and it was more than simply the music. "it became a cultural thing," he says. "You know, the hip-hop and rap artists and all that. As a kid you get this wild effect with nice cars and just anything that any kid goes through when they're seeing things being sensationalized."

One of the benefits of hip-hop music is that it does not necessarily require a large professional studio. Even many of the hit recordings in the early days had been made on fairly crude equipment. So for kids like Jason and Carl Martin it was a style of music that was not only enjoyable, it was also something that they could create themselves with little or no investment. Jason, Carl and another friend, Marcus Brown, became excited at the creative possibilities.

Teenaged Jason in his bedroom where he first began to develop his own beats

"That started to really take shape with Marcus and Carl," says Jason. "We wanted to do music and that's kind of where all the music came from. I was basically a DJ in high school and Marcus was a rapper and Carl was a rapper. Carl's mom, at the time, was doing a lot of vocal stuff as well. She had a lot of singing going on. Both Carl and his brother Derek were heavy into music. Carl had this other friend, Dwayne, and they were doing some things. We would go over to his house and they hovered around this one record player and they're just kind of creating beats. We were doing what we could as middle-class families to try to make things work and trying to fit the character as best as we could with the little money we had."

Like a lot of kids, Jason began to develop his DJ skills in his bedroom. "My mother had bought this little all-in-one stereo for me and looking back, you'd just chuckle to look at us!" he says. "Like something you'd buy at Sears and Roebuck! It wasn't intended to be like a mixing station, so to speak. But it had the radio and a connecting turntable on the top of it and cassette players; one of those all-in-one things, something you're Intended to put in the corner. But I wanted to be a DJ so I even had a piece of wood and I used stencils and I stenciled out 'Cut Master Jay.' That was the name I gave myself. Yeah, I remember that!"

Jason's fascination with the music, the hip-hop aura and the realization that he could create it himself, drove him to find ways to make it work to the best of his abilities, despite the limited resources.

"My mother kind of supported some of it," admits Jason. "The Kangol hats were coming out in style with Run DMC and all that. My mother didn't make much as a teacher, but she decided to buy this hat for me. It was like $90.00 at the time and she really wanted to kill me! But she knew that I would have people over and we're doing these mixes."

The sudden surge in popularity of Kangol hats must have surprised the manufacturer that had been in business since 1918. Or maybe not. They'd had a steady business for decades and Kangol hats were in every British gentleman's wardrobe. They even supplied berets for the British Army in World War II and had secured a contract in the 1960s to be the Beatles' 'official' headgear provider.

As hip hop grew in the 1980s, major clothing trends grew along with the culture, particularly styles worn by influential hip-hop artists. Numerous emcees – such as Run DMC – would be seen on stage and videos wearing Kangol hats that seem to emphasize their aura of cool. When LL Cool J wore a Kangol Bermuda Casual on an album cover, every b-boy had to sport a Kangol.

When the all-in-one stereo with one turntable wasn't enough to make the beats Jason wanted, it was time for an investment in some equipment.

"I think we went to RadioShack and I had like this little, very entry-level mixer and this other turntable," he says. "It was actually one of those turntables that had a speaker connected to it and it was very elementary."

The records took a beating, however. "I was using that to scratch with records and I was really messing up vinyl records because I didn't have Technics 1200s and all that. I mean I was going through records and it was really, really bad. But you're chasing your dreams, you're gonna do what you have to."

The lack of high-tech recording equipment wasn't really a roadblock.

Jason's early music collaborator Carl 'Groove' Martin who later founded the million-selling R&B vocal group Shai.

"It turns out we really started creating some things with just really, I mean, just 'nuts falling from the tree' if you will," he recalls with a degree of pride. "We were putting those things together and just making some things happen. We turned out a couple of songs that were just incredible at the time and so that's it. I learned how to DJ through that stuff that we kind of pieced together."

Jason remembers a song from back then that he and Carl put together. "I think it was called 'Down to the Rhythm,'" he recalls. "The reason I remember that was because there was a song that LL Cool J had made and he had a part in that song that went, 'Down to the rhythm that I rock the world,' and so I was basically mixing that in with Carl's voice because Carl would rap and then that became like a chorus line. That's kind of something we presented and actually gained some interest from some people in the industry. But, yeah, it was pretty exciting."

CHAPTER 12

Beating the Windmill

> *"He locked himself into a room for about a month and he did nothing but those moves until he figured it out."* – Carl Martin

AS NOTED ABOVE, break dancing was a major part of hip-hop culture, particularly in the 1980s and for Jason it presented a challenge that he was determined to conquer.

"There were some pretty early signs of Jason being different in a way," said Carl. "There were some break dance moves that none of us would attempt because we thought we would break our necks! But during that time early to mid-eighties, when dancing was everything, he locked himself into a room for about a month and he did nothing but those moves until he figured it out. Then he showed up at a skating rink with bandanas on his head, his neck, his elbows, his knees, to show you he could do it. I think he almost killed himself, but he was pretty determined. And then I saw him do the same thing with teaching himself how to DJ and I've seen him do this several times."

The memory of that episode has stayed with Marcus Lyle Brown, too. One of the specific dance moves was known as the Windmill and to be considered a true b-boy, you had to do the Windmill. At that time, it was rare to see a dancer perform the move faultlessly as it requires a high level of athleticism and co-ordination. It involves the dancer rolling on his chest, shoulders and back continuously in a circle on the floor while twirling his legs in the air. When performed flawlessly, it seems to defy the laws of physics, the body apparently driven by an unseen force, almost floating above the ground in a blend of strength and gracefulness. It's hard to do and easy to mess up but messing up wasn't an option for Jason.

"I see that incident with the Windmill as an example that if Jason sets his mind on executing something or solving a problem or pursuing an aspiration, to this day, he does so with a level of determination and tenacity that everyone can appreciate and leverage and benefit from, if they would apply that same level of determination," Marcus stipulated. "Of course, work ethic and passion have a lot to do with it, but at the end of the day, he never stopped, he never quit until he was satisfied with the outcome. He had told us he was going to do a Windmill and he kept practicing until he got it right. That personifies Jason. 'I'm gonna do it until I get it right.'"

Jason's friend Marcus Lyle Brown, now a noted
movie actor and producer.

Carl agreed. "That's how I look at his whole life," he said. "He wills himself into things."

"If I had to answer the question, 'What defines Jason and what brought him to his career path?' I really think that I would have to rest on determination," Marcus emphasized.

Jason didn't pursue music as a career but he didn't abandon it altogether, even creating a new 'stage name' to replace Cut Master Jay, as we shall see later.

For Carl 'Groove' Martin, his love of music developed into a career. He founded the R&B vocal group Shai, best known for their No. 1 hit single "If I Ever Fall In Love" that was certified double platinum and the album of the same name that he produced.

For Marcus Lyle Brown, rapping alongside Jason and Carl evolved into a career in the entertainment industry as he is now an accomplished movie actor who has already chalked up an impressive list of movie credits on the big screen and television. He also has a number of credits as a producer.

But all of that grew from the interest that Jason, Carl and Marcus shared in hip-hop as young teens in Lafayette.

CHAPTER 13

LSU from tryout to walk-on

"You hope that you don't have an off day, essentially, especially when you're trying out, you're auditioning. I knew it was all up to me." – Jason Cormier

THE SUMMER FOLLOWING High School graduation, Jason Cormier arrived at Louisiana State University's Baton Rouge campus for the first time as a student; marking a day he will never forget. He'd played for one of the most revered high school teams in Louisiana – St. Thomas More – and his sights were set on playing for the illustrious LSU team, with hopes of an NBA career beyond that.

On more than one occasion, scouts from what is now known as University of Louisiana at Lafayette (UL) had watched Jason play when he was at St. Thomas More, but LSU was where Jason was determined to go. Like all LSU fans, Jason would say, "I bleed purple and gold," a tradition that dates back to the 1890s.

"I mean LSU is like the flagship University here in Louisiana, so if you're a kid involved in any sort of sports then you bleed purple and gold," Jason points out. "Don't get me wrong, anyone would be lucky to attend the University of Louisiana just as well and there are many that bleed red and white just as much!" he adds, referring to UL's Ragin' Cajuns team colors.

Colleges, including LSU, will recruit high school basketball superstars, those rare individuals who will likely be part of the

LSU team. While recognized as a good player, Jason was not as naturally gifted as some of the other freshmen and he knew that his goal of being part of LSU's team would depend on more than just his talent. He would have to out-work everyone to even be considered for a place on the team.

"When I arrived, it was a little overwhelming," Jason acknowledges. "It's a big campus. It's a school I'd looked forward to attending. I wanted to play basketball and when I was at school, I used to stay up late nights and watch some of the guys playing basketball at LSU at the time. Ricky Blanton was one of them and Wayne Sims. And then, you know, seeing those guys on campus! Oh man! It was cool to actually be able to see them in person and then starting to hang out or going to the gym to work out with them and pick-up games and whatnot."

For twenty-five years, the LSU Tigers were coached by the legendary Dale Brown, known as 'The Master Motivator' for his ability to inspire his team to victory against higher-ranked opponents. He is also remembered by LSU fans for his so-called 'freak defense' that successfully confused the opposing team, often resulting in an unexpected win.

The 1980s were remarkable years for Brown who led the LSU Tigers twice to Final Four appearances. He was also known as a strong advocate for the rights of student athletes, particularly those who were in financial need.

From 1988 through the early 1990s, future NBA stars such as Chris Jackson (later known as Mahmoud Abdul-Rauf), Stanley Roberts and Dr. Shaquille O'Neal wore the purple and gold of the LSU Tigers.

Coach Brown remembers when he first met Jason Cormier.

"What I did each year, I would always have tryouts," said Coach Brown. "Now those tryouts didn't mean we were going to keep anybody, but a lot of times there's hidden kids in school that have a certain quality you need. I didn't keep a walk-on every year, but I did this one particular year."

A walk-on, Brown explained, refers to a student who is not receiving an athletic scholarship but tries out for the team and is given the opportunity to play.

"Sometimes we'd have 75 to maybe 100 kids try out, other years fewer numbers," Brown noted. "I don't remember how many tried out when Jason tried out, but there was something special about him. He just had an aura about him and I can't explain it. I didn't know anything about him."

Brown described how his process worked. "My one assistant usually would break them down until we had just a few left," he said, "then I'd go watch the last night and then make a decision with him. Well, we decided to keep Jason, and it's bizarre because I had really good luck in keeping walk-ons. In fact, in the twenty-five years I coached here, four of our players wound up being doctors. Three of those four were walk-ons. I don't know. I didn't have a crystal ball or could read the future in any way." Brown chuckled at the memory of his players who went on to become medical professionals.

Jason vividly recalls those LSU tryouts. "You don't know who you'll be up against in tryouts," he says. "I think they had almost a hundred people show up, it was packed! You go through a series of drills to see if you can at least handle the ball. Can you dribble it then can you shoot the ball, what can you actually do? That cut it down."

That preliminary part of the tryouts took up an entire morning. Jason's older brother John was there at the time and came to watch. One of John's good friends was also trying out at the same time.

Trying out for a place on a major college team, especially LSU, could be intimidating, but Jason had been focused on this opportunity since his early childhood. His endless practice in every kind of weather and his determination to perfect his every move gave him the confidence he needed to succeed at this crucial moment.

"Overall, I knew I had a lot of skills," he says, not bragging but as a simple matter of fact. "I wasn't really worried because I'd received offers from some other colleges, other schools out of state, not as big as LSU, but I really wanted to attend LSU. At the tryouts, it went from almost a hundred to forty or so pretty quickly, or whatever it was. Later, it had come down to five or six people and we all kind of played each other, one-on-one, in front of the coaches."

Jason recalls how the final choice was made. "Funnily enough, it came down to when I played against my brother's good friend who was a pretty bold trash talker. I mean it just wasn't really even fair. I just kind of did what I had to do and won."

Jason remembered that his brother John had talked about his friend's skillset and it could have been daunting to face him at the tryouts.

"I never really worried about it because you walk in and you know what you have and you're looking at other people and you're like, whatever! So it was good that my brother was there. I kinda had something to prove to my brother, and his friend just got spanked really bad. After that, I think he had played another guy that I was supposed to play the last match with and he had actually beat that guy. When I beat him so bad they said it wasn't even necessary to play the last match. They were like, 'No, that's good.' They chose me and this guy named Steven Ussery and they said, 'Welcome guys. Probably not a surprise but you guys have been selected,' and we got on the roster."

It may not have been exactly a surprise, but it was welcome news and a relief for Jason to know he'd made the cut.

"It's weird because you know what your skill set is and I knew I was deserving, but easily one of the greatest moments of my life, to play for Coach Dale Brown!" he acknowledges. "You hope that you don't have an off day, essentially, especially when you're trying out, you're auditioning. I knew it was all up to me."

Looking back, Jason thinks that his aura of self-confidence could have been misinterpreted during the tryouts. He recalls, "I think it was Coach Abernathy that said, 'There was just some concern that you kinda roll your eyes sometimes,' and I was like, 'Well, I mean, that's just kind of cockiness.' Everybody rolls their eyes like, 'You're like really gonna try to guard me?' So it was one of those things and I was hoping that it wouldn't go against me. It was just more of on-the-court showmanship. I didn't mean anything negative by it but it was like, 'Really? You're gonna try to guard me?'"

Fortunately, Jason's show of self-assurance did not go against him. "I guess Coach Brown had a feeling that came over him and he granted scholarships to two players, me and Steven Ussery."

Jason says that it felt "magnanimous" being granted that scholarship because, "Yeah, I'm really gonna wear the purple and gold! It was like my dream was coming true. That was overwhelming."

The LSU Tigers Yearbook 1989-1990.
Legendary Coach Dale Brown center; Jason Cormier far right.

CHAPTER 14

Life on and off the LSU court

"One of the things I liked about him, he never once ever complained about anything. When he went into a game, he went in with total confidence." – Coach Dale Brown

RECEIVING AN ATHLETIC SCHOLARSHIP, being part of the basketball program at LSU, was an achievement but it was only a start. "I was also trying to fit in," he says. "How do the athletes look? How do they interact with people? And here I was, this kid, I had some athleticism but at the same time I was always, I guess, groomed to have really good grades and that really wasn't the interpretation, the perception, of what the athletes were all about."

In fairness, he notes, many of the athletes worked hard on their academics despite the perception, but it was important for Jason, as one of the younger players, to be perceived as fitting in with the style and attitudes of the other athletes.

"There were these special lines for athletes, and it was quite intimidating, but right off the bat, the athletes were very welcoming," he notes. "Not only the basketball team but the football team as well. I would spend some time with Lyle Mouton who matriculated the year before me. He was a baseball and basketball standout, so I was able to stay at his apartment with two of the football players that he was roommates with and he helped with that transition a great deal."

That transition to life as a college athlete wasn't easy because Jason was one of the youngest freshmen at that time and he says that made a huge difference between him and the older athletes. For example, he says, "You can't go to the bars with them so that was a strike against you. Like, 'Hey, we're gonna go get a drink after' or whatever. I can't go, so that's automatically a strike against you."

After initially staying with Lyle Mouton off campus, Jason roomed with Marcus Brown, his former high school friend with whom he and Carl Martin had made their first venture into creating music.

"I remember a night when we were college roommates," recalled Marcus. "I was outside with Jason while he was working on the sound system in his car. Finally, I got tired and I said, 'I'm going in.' The next morning, I walked out into the parking lot, I could see his feet. His feet were on the headrests and he was upside down underneath the steering column, because that's where he needed to be in order to fix the sound system, to solve whatever problem there was. Literally, he was asleep upside down. He stopped right where he was."

Marcus believes that was a perfect example of Jason's attitude of focus and perseverance. "It was a visual illustration of him carrying something through to fruition," he said. "Jason did not stop until there was a smile on his face and that smile was that level of accomplishment or achievement: 'I did it. I figured it out. I'm done now.'"

Then in the second semester of his first year Jason was rooming with Dennis Tracey. "I had moved into the LSU dormitory, the actual athletic dormitory," says Jason. Now he felt like he was part of the team.

The Tigers had a strong roster of talent that year and it wasn't easy for Jason, as a walk-on, to get a lot of court time. "He just only played in six games that one year he was on the team," said

Brown. "He was on a good team. We won twenty games. We had a good solid basketball team but he always was the same. He just had a tenacity to him and he was a very bright player. He never did any stupid things. He just had good common sense."

Even on a team that strong, Jason made a lasting impression on the Tigers' head coach.

"One of the things I liked about him, in the limited time he played – as I said he only got in six games that year – but he never once ever complained about anything," he said. "When he went into a game, he went in with total confidence."

Brown made a point of adding, "It's nothing spectacular he ever did, but he was an ideal practice player because he came to practice every day and he knew he wasn't going to play a lot, obviously, because of the talent we had but he gave it his all. He was a quick learner, too."

Being a reliable team member, practicing… then practicing some more until every move becomes second nature. These are character traits developed in high school sports and while creating beats as a budding DJ and mastering dance moves that made him a valuable asset to the LSU Tigers. That 'total confidence' that Coach Brown remarked upon would become a key element of his skill set when he became a medical doctor and then a neurosurgeon. It would have served him equally well regardless of the career path he eventually chose.

"I'm not one bit surprised for him to become a brain surgeon," said Brown. "I could have never predicted that because how do you know what we're going to become? But I knew he'd be highly successful."

Brown remembers Jason's mother, too, calling her 'a special lady.' "The time she grew up in the Deep South was not a very good place to be because of all the racism, and she just defied that," said Brown. "She wasn't bitter. She's just a sweet lady, a strong lady, a bright lady."

Brown also revealed an unusual and unfortunate family background that he and Jason happen to share by coincidence. "I never really pushed Jason about his dad because I had the same thing happen to me," he disclosed. "Two days before I was born, my biological father abandoned my mother and me and never, ever came back."

Despite the lack of a father figure in their lives, both men went on to achieve remarkable careers: Dale Brown with more than a quarter of a century leading the LSU Tigers, and Jason Cormier becoming a renowned neurosurgeon and entrepreneur.

Jason and Coach Brown stay in touch, attending team reunions and meeting some of the current players, too. "And when we have reunions, guess who always comes dressed very dignified? It's Jason Cormier," says Brown. "And guess who the kids go talk to, the superstars? They'll go talk to Jason Cormier!"

Thinking back to the day that Jason showed up as one of many hopefuls with the dream of playing for the LSU Tigers, Brown said, "You know, for him, first of all, to have the courage to come out and try out for basketball..." Not a lot of kids would have that degree of resolution.

Over the decades, Coach Brown has worked with and mentored young men of every personality type and differing athletic ability. "I see why he is a brain surgeon with his confidence," he said. "He never gets rattled, never gets too high, never gets too low. Just a good solid man. We need more Jason Cormiers in the world."

When Jason thinks back to those first two years at LSU, he has some mixed emotions. On the plus side, he had defied the odds, being selected as a walk-on, joining teammates who were there on athletic scholarships. He had achieved that by a sheer determination to succeed and accepting only the best from himself. He had been coached by the legendary Dale Brown, playing in major college arenas in games broadcast on national TV alongside players that would go on to become stars in the NBA.

Jason on the court again, participating in an LSU Alumni game

On the downside, he admits that he was allowing his level of scholastic achievement to slide.

"My initial time at LSU, when I first started, my mindset was like a lot of other athletes in that I was going to play a couple of years and then make the jump to the NBA," he says. "I mean, that was my dream."

With his focus set firmly on constantly improving his game, academics took a back seat. Additionally, Jason was beginning to experience pain in his lower back. He ignored it for a while, but soon it was apparent that he was suffering from muscle spasms in the lower back. It's a condition that can be the result of injuries to the muscles, tendons and ligaments in the back. Sports – particularly those that involve turning the back suddenly and repeatedly – can aggravate the condition. For Jason, the symptoms ranged from mild discomfort to chronic spasms with severe pain that made it difficult to move. He would sometimes ease the discomfort by sleeping on the floor rather than in bed.

"Yeah, I was an active player the first year and then I developed muscle spasms in my lower back and that kind of put me out," he says now with some regret. "And so I went on a… I guess it's a medical scholarship, essentially. You can't go back from a medical scholarship to an athletic scholarship."

Jason's cousin, Royale Colbert, believed he knew the origin of Jason's back problems, dating back to his high school sports. "Jason hit a ball with so much torque – this is my uneducated guess – that's probably how he injured his back. Because, I mean, he would hit a baseball so hard and so far and so accurately. I remember that was when he first had some issues with his back."

Jason's mother remembers him suffering both the pain from the spasms and the anguish of being off the team. "LSU went to the NCAA tournament and he couldn't travel with the team," she said. "I'll never forget, he was in the den and looking at his team playing in El Paso and it broke my heart seeing him sitting there like that. He really, really, really loved basketball."

No longer on the team, he finished out the year but could not completely forget about basketball. He says, "I decided I wanted to continue to chase this dream and I made the jump and I went to Spain."

CHAPTER 15

Shooting hoops in Spain

"It was an opportunity, and I was going to chase it, no matter what." – Jason Cormier

IT WAS QUITE A JUMP. For Jason, still a teenager, it was an adventure and an opportunity he couldn't turn down: playing pro or semi-pro basketball in Europe. Looking back, Jason feels it wasn't that hard a decision to make when an agent approached him with an attractive offer.

"They have agents crawling all over universities," he notes. "I was contacted like every athlete is. I mean I was contacted and just had some discussions and they said, 'Hey, you want to come to try out?' so I did and they said, 'We want to bring you in.'"

A contributing factor to his decision may have been that Jason and his mother were not on good terms and with his father long gone, the decision was his alone.

"At the time, I really wasn't talking to my mother," he points out. "She just kind of refused to hear anything. I was still kind of upset about how everything went down and all that was still kind of fresh. I ended up having to sign my power of attorney, essentially a guardianship, to an agent. And that's how I was able to go to Spain. It was scary but at the same time I wanted to play basketball."

Jason had to rely on his agent as something of a substitute parent while he was in Spain, as part of La Federacion Internacional de Baloncesto (FIBA), 1991 – 1993. The agent helped Jason acquire a passport, took care of the travel documents and other legal issues as well as arranging living accommodations.

Until then, Jason had grown up with family and friends he'd known almost all his life. He'd been in a familiar environment, playing basketball in high school in Lafayette and at LSU in Baton Rouge. Now he would fly to Europe to live with and play basketball with people he didn't know.

"There were a lot of American players down there that had played college ball here in the States," he says, "But you don't know who they are unless you've come across them at something like a five-star camp before playing college ball or even in summer league, but yeah, you don't know anybody."

For the most part, says Jason, his relationship with his agent worked out okay. "I understood it was a guy that made some money off the deal and in the end that's what they want," he acknowledges. "But at the time, you're thinking, 'Man, I'm just going to live my dream and see what happens.' It was an opportunity, and I was going to chase it, no matter what."

In retrospect, Jason thinks maybe the agent might have made more from the deal than he should have. "I didn't really understand the numbers at the time," he admits. "For example, calling internationally, after I kind of got homesick a little bit. My cell phone bills were crazy, like $10,000 or $12,000 because you're calling internationally so that's kind of what drove me back. I was like, 'Man, it's just crazy!' But your agent's like, 'Well, you're spending this money,' but you don't know. And at the end of the month, you're like, 'This is what's left? Wait, What?'"

But, as Jason points out, he was young. "Your agent is like your best friend and your guardian, so I didn't know any better. But in the end, it provided me with a new perspective on the world. That experience helped me in many different ways, so I think it was worth it."

For Jason, playing in Spain was definitely a different experience to playing college ball in the U.S. "I mean, you're playing in different countries, you're traveling, but it's not the same," he explains. "It's fun but it's just not what you grew up with. You are not wearing, maybe, New York Knicks across your back, you're not wearing the 76ers across your shirt, across your chest, you're not wearing LSU Tigers' colors. It's just different; it's not the same."

He remembers one particular aspect that made it different. "You're playing in pavilions that are open, so while you're shooting basketball there are birds flying through the pavilion. It's kinda weird! It's cool and it's still a lot of talent, a whole lot of talent, but it's very different. It's not NBA or NCAA ball."

Eventually, life on the basketball courts of Europe began to lose its appeal. For Jason there was one added advantage: "I was able to get out, too."

That wasn't always the case for players who signed on with overseas programs. "There are some people down there, friends I know, that can't get out," he reveals, "But that wasn't me. I mean, I still had my mother and about that point in time we kind of started talking again and I decided maybe I should go home, stay stateside and buckle down and get back to school."

CHAPTER 16

The road back to LSU

"Working there, doctors just became my heroes." – Jason
Cormier

JASON RETURNED FROM SPAIN, having played almost two years of pro
basketball in Europe. He had proved to himself that he could do it
by focusing on a goal and doing whatever it took to achieve it.

Perhaps his time overseas helped him to redirect his focus to
another vocation where he could achieve success. In any case, he
realized that job number one was to work on his education if he
was to have any chance of succeeding in any endeavor.

For Jason, returning to LSU was almost like starting over. "I
had to redo some things because in my first year, I hadn't applied
myself," he admits candidly. "My perception at that time was, I'm
not trying to be the nerd of the basketball team, so I was just kind
of, whatever, and made some piss-poor grades."

Jason had found that it was easy to let the grades slip, even
though he had proved at high school that he was capable of
achieving good grades. But as he had said, it was his desire to 'fit
in' with the lifestyle of his fellow athletes that led him to ignore
his classroom studies. There was a perception that athletes didn't
need to worry too much about that kind of thing.

"That was my own perception," he stipulates, "And I don't
want to insult the guys who were really trying, because that's not
what LSU was based on. I mean, as athletes, we had tutors and

all that. We had opportunities to study. Some of us, we just didn't. I mean, it was like fun time."

Having said that, Jason recognizes that the LSU athletic program continues to maintain one of the highest grade point averages in the SEC, well above 3.0 GPA.

"When I had initially started at LSU, I didn't care. Academics was like the last thing on my mind. I was like, I'm going to go there and play a couple of years and head for the NBA. That was it. I grew up watching Julius Erving, Magic Johnson, Larry Bird, and all those people, and I was like, 'One day I'm going to play against them.'"

Returning to LSU, Jason got back on track. "I had to go back and do some things. I met with Mike Mallett who was over the academic center. He told me that LSU had this ninth semester scholarship that they provided for athletes to finish out their academics. That helped a lot, and Coach Brown signed off on it. That helped me get back to focusing and doing what I needed to do and ultimately, obviously, strengthen my academics and finish out."

He began working towards a degree in zoology and botany. He realized he was going to have to work his way through school. One of the jobs he took on was as a transporter at a hospital in Baton Rouge. As a transporter, Jason became familiar with every part of the hospital.

"They would call us and basically, this patient needs to go from their room to radiology, or whatever," he says. It was a fairly low-level job, but Jason found that he quickly became fascinated with what was happening at the hospital. "Working there, doctors just became my heroes," he says.

Working as a transporter, Jason got to wear the blue bootees and a scrub shirt. He was beginning to feel like this was where he belonged.

There was one place that seemed off-limits to a transporter: the operating room. "There were these doors off to the right at the end of this hallway on the second floor," he recalls. "And from the elevator, when we brought patients up, we would always turn left. But the door to the right, it was, like, 'The Forbidden Door.' Surgery! And I was like, 'Man! What goes on behind those doors? If I could just get a peek in there! That's where it happens!'"

It became a goal for Jason to see what went on behind 'The Forbidden Door' if only he could find a way to make it happen.

One day, Jason was in the hallway, looking down the corridor towards the operating room when a hospital staff member that he knew came by. "I asked him, 'Man, how do I get to work in surgery? Do you need, like, some sort of advanced degree?' Because I was still in college and just working as a transporter. He said, 'No, I'll put in a good word for you and just go ahead and apply.' And I said, 'Man! Really? Okay!'"

Jason seized the opportunity and immediately applied. "The lady's name was Genie Woodring. I called her and she said, 'Well, come on in for an interview,' and I was, like, 'What!' I was just a simple transporter. I had a pager on my hip. I thought it was the best thing in the world. I was wearing shoe covers, the whole nine! I was like living the dream already and I'm just a peon transporter, I'm not doing anything."

Jason was determined to make a good impression. "So I met with her and I was dressed up," he says. "Most of these guys, as I know now, would show up for their interviews in jeans and a tee shirt because it was an ancillary job. I showed up in a nice sweater, a tie and all that, and she was looking at me like, 'Okay, you know what you're applying for? You're not applying for medical school or anything.' We were talking, and she asked, 'What kind of experience do you have?' I said, 'I'm a transporter, I'm in school, I want to go to med school,' and one thing and another."

His admiration for doctors – particularly surgeons – had given him a new goal to aim for: going to med school and becoming a surgeon.

He must have impressed Ms. Woodring. She told Jason, "Look, I don't have anything right now, but who knows? Something might show up tomorrow, the next day, the next week. I'll let you know."

Again, Jason's single-minded persistence would pay off. "The next two weeks, I called her every single day," he says. "Every single day! She was like, 'This kid here, I mean there's something wrong with him. He's got no idea what he's fishing for.' I don't know if I was like the bill collector who wouldn't go away, but eventually, she said, 'Come on in and I'll find a job for you. You really want this.'"

CHAPTER 17

Going behind the 'Forbidden Door'

*"The word got around that he was a doctor in Baton Rouge.
I knew better, but the girls on the LSU campus all thought
that Jason was a doctor! He had the car, he had the scrubs,
he wore the lab coat!"* – Troy Melancon

HE'D FINALLY GOT HIS foot in the door: the 'Forbidden Door' that
he had passed so often while pushing gurneys and carts. He was
able to see what really happened in the O.R.

"I got in there and started to interact with the doctors and I
was getting exposed to it," he says. "I was looking at different operations and procedures and I was thinking, 'Well, I can do this!
This isn't so esoteric or so high above my aptitude that I can't
achieve this.' And so, more and more, I started to see heart surgeons, I started to see orthopedic surgeons, I started to see
neurosurgeons. And I was like, 'Okay. Yes, I can do this.' It was
that exposure that did it for me."

Jason became totally convinced that he needed to attend med
school and become a surgeon. "One of the things I appreciated
was – being a transporter in the operating room – when the E.R.
would call, it was always a trauma or something. You'd go down
there and you'd see so many different things. But the surgeons,
on the other hand, were in a situation where they could give a
patient a second chance. With seconds left, they were saving
lives."

His long-time friend James Ambroise remembers seeing him back then. "He was at LSU and I would go and visit with him and some other friends," he recalls. "He'd say, 'Yeah, I've been working, I've got to go to work and be in surgery, helping out in surgery.' We all always used to think, 'Man, you're crazy! You're not actually going to work in surgery!'"

Troy Melancon, another of Jason's friends from high school, had gone on to play pro baseball in the minor leagues before settling on a career as a nurse anesthetist. He too remembers those days.

"So, here was Jason, who I didn't know was working as a scrub tech in the hospital in Baton Rouge and I was in New Orleans at the time," says Troy. "Every time I saw him, he was in scrubs and a lab coat. The word got around that he was a doctor in Baton Rouge. I knew better, but the girls on the LSU campus all thought that Jason was a doctor! He had the car, he had the scrubs, he wore the lab coat!"

Looking back with the benefit of hindsight, Jason says, "It makes sense now. I was trying to make ends meet, of course; being a college student and all that. But I basically outfitted myself to look like an aspiring doctor, a surgeon or whatever you want to call it because I not only wore scrubs, but I had shoe covers on, I purchased a pager, I was paying for a pager account. I thought I was ready. This is the big league. I would wear a surgery cap and I know people looked at me like, 'You're just nuts!' But I was like, 'Man! I feel important!' I'm feeling like, you know, they need me at the hospital. This is what it's all about. But I was just a transporter. It wasn't like I was a doctor or anything like that."

Some people might describe Jason's actions as 'fake it till you make it' or what might be called an 'act as if' attitude. In her book *The Secret*, author Rhonda Byrne put it this way: "How do you get yourself to a point of believing? Start make-believing. Act as if you have it already. As you make-believe, you will begin to believe you have received."

Jason saw himself as a doctor. All he had to do was to make that a reality.

CHAPTER 18

Sights set on the O.R.

> *"I had to go back and re-do some of the academic courses*
> *that were below medical school appeal, so that I could prove*
> *that now I was a different person to the one I'd been before."*
> – Jason Cormier

TROY MELANCON, WHO HAD seen Jason impressing the ladies around the Baton Rouge campus in his scrubs, was unaware that Jason truly had his sights set on a medical career, until he received a memorable phone call from him. "One day he calls me up in a serious manner, and he says, 'Troy, I want to go to medical school.' And I was like, 'Dude, you need to use your prowess from LSU, all the years of sports you gave them, and get your butt into medical school.'" Troy would prove to be a true friend, helping and encouraging Jason on his journey to becoming a doctor.

It was hard work. He had to catch up on a lot of course work that he had let slip previously. He had to get his grades up to par in order to achieve the bachelor's degree, a must-have first step if he was to qualify for a place at med school.

"I had to go back and re-do some of the academic courses that were below medical school appeal, so that I could prove that now I was a different person to the one I'd been before," says Jason. "Back then I was really just a derelict and now I'm really focused, and this is what I want."

It was while he was an undergrad at LSU that Jason met Dallas Webb who would become a life-long friend.

"I remember the exact moment I met Jason," said Dallas. "We were in a parasitology class and the professor basically said, 'Okay, everybody needs to pair up to be lab partners.' I had moved down to Louisiana from Connecticut, so I didn't know anybody at LSU and I was way out of my element in terms of culture. I mean from Connecticut to Baton Rouge is a big step."

Most of the other students knew each other and easily paired up as lab partners.

"I just remember walking out of the class just like I don't know anybody," said Dallas. "I was trying to find somebody that was still available. Jason came up to me and said, 'Hey, do you have a partner?' and the rest is history. We just hit it off from then and it was good. We've been best friends, brothers, ever since. God put him in my life, I know that."

Although their careers would keep them both extremely busy, working in different cities – Dallas is now a portfolio manager for a fund that invests in biotechnology companies – they remain close.

"Jason was the best man at my wedding," said Dallas. "We've never lost touch. I would say there's an unspoken bond there that if either of us ever picked up the phone and said, 'Hey bro, I need you,' the other one would be on a plane immediately. There's no doubt about that."

In addition to his studies, Jason was often working two jobs – including his work as a transporter at the hospital – in order to stay in college. Friends and fellow students commented that he seemed to go for days with little or no sleep, going from classes to study halls to his paying jobs. He was driven by his determination to reach his goal.

"I'm studying, I'm going to work," he says. "I'm trying to sneak around and study while I'm at work at the hospital as a transporter.

I was basically getting maybe, *maybe* an hour, an hour-and-a-half of sleep per night, maybe that, and my coffee consumption went up significantly."

It was taking a toll on Jason's health.

"One morning, I was found at the bottom of the stairs at the stairwell in my apartment," he says frankly. "The air conditioner was off because I wouldn't really run my air conditioning much at all, just trying to save money and studying and just doing things. It was kind of just a survival thing and trying to make smart decisions. I think the combination of the heat and lack of sleep just hit me all at once. It was basically I just passed out. I think they thought I fell on the stairs or something."

The hard work was paying off and in 1996, Jason received a BSc degree in zoology and had his sights set on progressing to medical school. Despite the grueling schedule he could see the light at the end of the tunnel and had rededicated himself to academic excellence.

Jason was ready to move forward and apply for admission to med school. Part of the application process involves taking the Medical College Admission Test, known as MCAT, devised by the Association of American Medical Colleges (AAMC). The MCAT is a standardized, multiple-choice, computer-based test that has been a part of the medical school admissions process for more than 90 years. Each year, more than 85,000 students take the exam.

Jason took the MCAT with the intention of applying to study medicine at LSU. However, right at that time, Fate stepped in and changed the lives of Jason and his family with terrible, traumatic results. Jason's younger brother Jeremiah, known to friends and family as Jerry, was tragically killed in an automobile accident.

Even today, Jerry's death is a subject that is almost too painful for Jason and his family to talk about. Jason's friend, Carl Martin,

*Jason Cormier receives his Bachelor of Science degree
from Louisiana State University.*

remembers the horrific incident. "Jerry died in a car accident," said Carl, "And it occurred when he was actually driving down the street that they lived on. They lived kind of on the main thoroughfare that he was on and I think they estimated he was going about 130 mph when he got into the accident."

Jason's cousin Royale recalled that the car was a Nissan 300

ZX. "John had two of them and the first one he got, he gave to Jason," Royale explained. "Jason was mature enough to drive the car. It was a sports car; very, very fast. Then John got another one and when he got ready to buy another car he gave that one to Jerry. So Jeremiah had a car just like Jason but the problem was Jeremiah wasn't mature enough to drive the car. They don't talk about it because Jason had told John. 'Jerry is not ready for that car yet.' Jason always says, 'I told John not to give Jerry that car.' But again, you have to recognize Jason was always the more mature among them because he was always the more grounded."

Jason's maturity made him a more capable driver. "Jason knew, 'If I turn this car at ninety-nine miles an hour, it's going to flip,'" said Royale. "And Jason had told John that Jeremiah was not ready for that yet. John was like, 'Well you got one, he can have one.' I remember this conversation distinctly. Jason said, 'No John, he's not ready for that.' And John did it anyway, so there's always been that issue between the two brothers."

Understandably, Jason was deeply affected by the tragedy. "I went through a lot of depression after my brother passed away," he says. "I was angry with God, I was angry with just the whole situation."

In the depths of depression, even his excitement about a medical career seemed to fade in importance as he struggled with the loss of his brother. "I was angry with just good people being taken away. I really kind of looked in depth into what I felt. I went through a lot of spiritual challenges internally and so I pulled my application."

Eventually, Jason began to find his way back on track, intellectually and spiritually. "I took this comparative religion course at LSU and I think that was part of what helped me get out of it," he says.

As he began to pick up the pieces, he renewed his belief that becoming a surgeon would be his way to offer other people hope and the gift of returning to a fulfilling life. He knew the only med school he wanted to attend was LSU.

CHAPTER 19

Words of wisdom

"Only you, yourself, can keep you out of medical school." –
Dr. Sam McCluggage

"TROY MELANCON WAS IN New Orleans and he was a nurse about to start nurse anesthetist school at that time," Jason recalls. "I reached out to him and I said, 'Hey, I'm coming to New Orleans, would you like to hang out,' etcetera, and he's like, 'Oh man, great.' He was very hospitable."

Jason was heading to New Orleans with a specific purpose in mind. Earlier, he had met with Dr. Allen Copping who was the Chancellor of the LSU Medical Center at the time. Dr. Copping knew that Jason had been in the athletic program and the reasons why his earlier grades had suffered but could also see that his current academic achievements were far better. He listened as Jason described his burning desire to become a surgeon. He could see that Jason was sincere and determined to succeed. At the end of their discussion, Dr. Copping said, "I'm going to get you in to speak with Dr. McCluggage, the Assistant Dean of Admissions at LSU."

In New Orleans, Troy dropped Jason off at the Admissions office with some words of encouragement. It was to be one of the most vital meetings of Jason's life.

Dr. Sam McCluggage and Jason had a frank and in-depth meeting. Finally, Dr. McCluggage leaned forward and gave him some advice he would never forget.

"Don't let anything or anyone stop you from going to medical school," he told Jason. "Don't let women do it, don't let distractions do it. Only you, yourself, can keep you out of medical school. Focus and think of it like you're on the basketball court, training."

As he left the meeting, Jason knew that it had been a good, positive conversation. If the meeting had gone badly, it could have spelled the end of Jason's dream of becoming a surgeon. At the very least, says Jason, "It wasn't a door-slam saying, 'You can't get in, think of something else.' It was more, 'Look, we're going to give you this opportunity but you need to put yourself in a position to matriculate to Medical School.' Dr. McCluggage told me I needed to take some more courses and enter a post-baccalaureate program."

Troy picked Jason up after the meeting and asked how it went. "He was really excited for me," says Jason. "He was like, 'Man, how do you feel? What happened?' He had a genuine interest, and I told him what Dr. McCluggage had told me to do and Troy said, 'Look, when they tell you this, do it. Just do it and just continue to push hard and Man, it's gonna be yours!' He had a genuine excitement for it."

The 'postbaccalaureate' program that Dr. McCluggage recommended is a course that students take after they have completed an undergraduate degree, designed specifically to support the transition to a professional school – such as med school – and enhances an applicant's competitiveness for admission.

Jason recognizes the positive role that Dr. McCluggage played in his medical career. "I became like his adopted son," he says, "And eventually his son would follow me at UAB and he's become a neurosurgeon. Dr. McCluggage did a lot for me."

Jason took Dr. McCluggage's words to heart. With renewed focus, he took two additional undergraduate degrees, giving him in total a BSc in Zoology/Botany with a minor in Chemistry and a BSc in Microbiology.

The result: "I reapplied," he says, "And I got into med school at LSU New Orleans."

CHAPTER 20

The reality of med school

"[Jason] went out of his way to help his fellow students. Everybody's competing for grades and things like that, but he was always the one that wanted to make sure everybody was learning and doing well." – Dani Bidros, MD

JASON CORMIER WAS BACK at Louisiana State University, but this time it was the New Orleans campus, not Baton Rouge. And now his focus was on the initials "MD" rather than "NBA" with the goal of becoming a medical doctor and progressing to the higher designation of surgeon. His previous work at the Baton Rouge hospital, first as a lowly transporter and then as a scrub tech, had instilled in him a burning desire to be working behind the 'Forbidden Door' but as a surgeon, leading his team and changing – even saving – the lives of his patients.

Jason was now at LSU's med school, officially known as Louisiana State University School of Medicine, having completed his pre-med and achieving BSc degrees in Microbiology and Zoology/Botany with a minor in Chemistry.

Unlike his first stint at LSU where he had arrived as a freshman with some of his friends from high school, going to med school was much more of a solo project.

"I had no idea of who was going to be there or any students from my pre-med," Jason recalls. But in any case, he had made up his mind that he was not there to make friends or socialize and party. Something of an introvert by nature, Jason didn't go out of his way to communicate with many of his fellow students on a social basis. "I was working two jobs – and at one point three jobs – and then going home and studying, so I really didn't have time to socialize or do anything like that," he says. "It was all business."

But it was a business he wanted to be fully immersed in and he was ready for the work that he knew it would take.

"I was focused, and I was a little bit older than at least some of those other students," he notes. Unlike some of his fellow incoming medical students, Jason had been through some life experiences – including a couple of years in Europe playing basketball – that the others may not have been exposed to.

"I was really ready for it and I was just ready to go," he says. Comparing the experience to entering the basketball arena, he says, "It was like starting another game."

Right from the get-go, Jason planned to live in a dormitory. "I did not want to have the stress of driving from an off-campus residence to the school," he explains. "I wanted to make sure I didn't have to deal with traffic or anything like that on an exam day or making excuses for being tired or not going in on time. I wanted it to be 100% at school. It was a full-time deal and basically all I had to do was walk across this bridge and I was in school. It was like a boarding school for me, essentially."

There wasn't a lot of time for relaxation, but Jason's cousin Royale recalled a time when the two of them stayed up thirty-six hours straight playing video games.

"He was at LSU and I was in law school there," said Royale. "The Xbox had just come out. We plug it in and we're like, 'We've got to study but we're just going to take a break.' We're studying and then we play the game one time and the game beats us. At that point, he starts trying to figure out why the game beat us. Thirty-six hours later, we had finally finished the game and we're looking at each other. We hadn't slept, we hadn't really eaten anything, but we'd finished. So he unplugs the game, puts it back in the box and it sits there for about three years.

"We were talking about it one day and I was like, 'Bro, we played video games for thirty-six hours.' He said, 'Yeah, but we beat the game.' I was like, 'Well Jason, that's not the point. The point is we wasted thirty-six hours.' His point was, 'But we *won*.' I could not make him understand that we had wasted thirty-six hours. His mindset was, 'We said we were gonna win and we won.' That's all he concentrated on. We said we were going to win and we had to win. I mean, that's just him. He needed to know how he won, what it took to win the game."

The learning curve at med school is necessarily steep right from the start. "It was didactic immediately," he notes about his first year at med school. "We had gross anatomy, really, that started early. There were some courses that were only in the classroom like emergency medicine and then we had seminars but primarily everything was didactics."

'Didactic' is a phrase commonly used in medical training to differentiate it from clinical demonstrations involving patients. These basics, says Jason, were primarily, "hitting home key points of gross anatomy and learning the baseline normalities of the human body."

Back when Jason was a hospital transporter and had found his way into the O.R., he had realized that this was something that wasn't beyond his capabilities. Now that was beginning to come to fruition.

"I was kind of far ahead of a number of people when it came to gross anatomy," he says, "because of my experiences at the Baton Rouge hospital. I really credit a number of the people I worked with at Baton Rouge General Medical Center for those experiences because it helped me move forward ahead of a number of people from Day One."

Gross anatomy, in medical terms, refers to the study of the biological structures of the human body that can be seen with the naked eye, rather than by other means such as a microscope or 'invasive' measures.

One of Jason's fellow students was Dani Bidros who met Jason for the first time at med school. "We're both from the same town and all these years later, we're still the best of friends," said Dani. "Right away, he was somebody that caught your eye; like when you spoke to him and how he carried himself."

Dani recalled that in their first year of medical school, one of the first courses they were introduced to was gross anatomy where they would dissect cadavers of human beings.

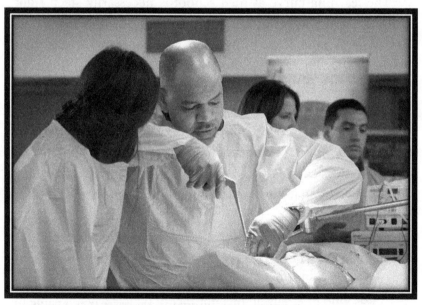

Passing on the knowledge years later: Dr. Cormier teaching students during a cadaver lab at the yearly World Congress for the Society of Brain Mapping and Therapeutics.

"That's kind of a big deal as far as life in medical school," Dani noted. "But oftentimes Jason would be helping other students.

Maybe he was a little bit more advanced, and this is a difficult subject, but he went out of his way to help his fellow students. Everybody's competing for grades and things like that, but he was always the one that wanted to make sure everybody was learning and doing well. That also brought me to appreciate him more."

Jason and Dani – now Dr. Dani Bidros – were the only two of their class of 180 at LSU med school that would go on to become neurosurgeons. They both returned to practice in their home town of Lafayette.

Jason realized that many of the other first-year medical students had not had the kind of involvement that he had already experienced. "Some of them came from medical families so they might have had those experiences of rounding or going to see patients in the hospital or shadowing in offices with their relatives," he acknowledges. "I didn't have that, so being able to be immersed in the atmosphere, as I had in Baton Rouge, made it a reality. When I got there, to medical school, I knew what I wanted to do."

Being in this environment had an exhilarating effect on Jason: "I felt, 'this is definitely my calling.'"

CHAPTER 21

Standing up to the rumor mill

"Why don't we have a little circle and we'll just talk anatomy and we'll see who knows what, because I've helped all of you in gross anatomy." – Jason Cormier

HOWEVER, AS AN AFRICAN AMERICAN in a predominantly white educational facility, he and other Black students could be the object of negative bias.

"The first year, I didn't realize that med school could be very similar to high school," says Jason, and he doesn't necessarily mean that in a good way. "There was just a lot of chatter and rumors and different things that would go around a classroom that you would not expect to find at a professional school. And this goes on across the country. It wasn't just limited to my school."

Regrettably, he found that race was at the root of the rumors that were circulating. "There were some racial issues there. There was some talk that the minority students were given access to tests in advance, that we were being given test questions that were going to be on the actual examination."

Then there were whispers circulating that 'special reviews' would take place for minorities prior to the actual exams. "That created a huge rift," says Jason.

There were only a small number of minorities, at least African American minorities, there, but the rumors began looming in the first semester. "It kind of pushed me away from the class," Jason admits, "because I met a bunch of people, some really good friends that I'm good friends with today. One of them I became very close to is Dani Bidros and I am the godfather to his daughter Isabella.

"But there were a number of guys that I met right up front and we played football together and it was good. It was great to be welcomed, but at the same time, it hit me like a sledgehammer when we found out some of these rumors were going around and some of the people that we thought were our friends were actually some of the people that were also spreading those rumors, to the point where I had considered transferring."

He is adamant about one thing: LSU was definitely not feeding any advance knowledge of test questions or answers to Black students and was not providing any preferential treatment to give minorities an unfair advantage.

"The school definitely didn't do that," he stipulates. "It was just chatter that was going on among the students. Just some ignorant students started spreading these rumors. It was born out of ignorance and there was obviously some envy and jealousy and, I guess, some discriminatory features about them, some deep things that I guess they needed to deal with."

Jason decided to take a proactive stance. "Some of them I confronted face-to-face. What's ironic is, some of those students, I had actually helped them with their dissection in the gross anatomy lab."

When Jason confronted three or four of them, they started telling on each other, more like school kids than medical students. "They started giving names of this person and that person and 'he said this and he said that' and so on," he says.

Jason had a challenge for them: "I said, 'Why don't we have a little circle and we'll just talk anatomy and we'll see who knows what, because I've helped all of you in gross anatomy. I can't believe that you guys will continue to say that knowing what I've done for you all.' It was very hurtful."

Dr. Sam McCluggage, as an effective leader, had something of a sixth sense when it came to feeling there was a hidden problem. "He's been really like my surrogate father, so he knew something was wrong," says Jason. "I mean, he was the guy that would see me in the hallway and walk up to me and talk to me and put his arm around me, so he knew something was wrong. When I finally told him, he was really appalled and really upset and demanded that there be some changes in the system and some sensitivity that needed to be highlighted in the system."

Dr. McCluggage took steps to ensure that African American students were more involved in decision-making positions. As part of that strategy, he appointed Jason to committees that could institute changes for the better.

One of those was the Admissions Committee that provides an important service for both the school and prospective students. As a member of this committee, Jason would read applications, interview prospective students and help make acceptance decisions. He was able to reflect on his own experiences and answer questions about life in med school. Additionally, when LSU began the process of recruiting a new Dean of Admissions for the School of Medicine, Jason was selected as one of only two students to sit on that committee.

Jason recognizes the influence that Dr. McCluggage was able to exert. "He really put forth a great deal of effort because he always strove for and stressed equality and all those sorts of things for everyone," he says.

Despite those efforts, there was never a return to a completely 'normal' atmosphere, whatever that was. "I was appreciative of what Dr. McCluggage did, but it was never really normal," says Jason. "It was more, 'I'm here and this is what I'm going to do and it's only going to be three more years.'"

Looking back, Jason is both philosophical and realistic about the situation. "I think that you can't mandate that people treat others fairly or look at people the same way," is how he puts it. "That has to be a decision between all of the people that are involved in the situation. It's like anything else. You can pass laws, but the laws can't make you look at a person as your equal."

By now, Jason had decided that nothing was going to derail him from achieving his goal.

"I was pretty focused so really that was the only thing in my life," he concedes. "It had become like tunnel vision for me. I was really going to focus just on medicine, so I guess I was lucky in that respect. I had the support of my family. At the time I wasn't speaking to my mother the first year I was at med school. We had kind of just gone our separate ways. My brother John was probably my biggest supporter along with my sister.

"I had made up my mind long ago that this was a journey. I knew that God was always going to be in my corner, so if I failed it was on me."

CHAPTER 22

Reaching back with a helping hand

"It's amazing how he could turn that focus switch on and he could be locked in on something for hours at a time, for days at a time." – Otis Drew, MD

SUCCESSFULLY COMPLETING HIS COURSE work at the end of his first year, Jason moved on to begin his second year at med school. It was then that he volunteered to meet with the incoming class of freshmen.

"Whenever you had incoming students in the next class – and LSU did a good job of this – a few weeks before school started or in the summertime, they would have a pre-matriculation type of seminar for minorities," says Jason. "They would come in and we would talk about what their experiences might be and how they could survive in a pool like this."

One of those incoming medical students was Otis Drew who immediately was struck by something about Jason.

"He kind of had this – can I put it this way – bravado about him that you could sense. I didn't know for sure, but I could sense that he was more than likely doing extremely well in medical school," said Otis. "Actually, he was very pivotal in the way that I performed in medical school, because I did extremely well as well, and he just kind of gave me a lot of guidance along the way."

Dr. Otis Drew is now an orthopedic surgeon with his own

practice in Lafayette, LA, and is also team doctor for the Ragin' Cajuns at the University of Louisiana.

These meetings with incoming students serve an important purpose, in Jason's opinion. "Arriving there, everyone's a little afraid because now the playing field is flat," he points out. "Everyone there is smart. There are no dummies."

While they were at high school and probably during their undergrad years at college, they stood out from the crowd as high achievers, but now each of them is just one of many high achievers.

"You've been told your entire life that you're the smartest person alive and that's intimidating because now you're at med school and there's a potential you could fail out even though you're smart," he says bluntly. "And then you have those rumors about 'You get this treatment, you get that treatment. This test is hard. You're gonna fail this, you're gonna fail that.' So, there's a lot of trepidation going in just because you hear all these stories about ten to fifteen people in the class are going to fail out or there are suicide attempts, all these sorts of things."

Meetings like this can reduce the level of intimidation for incoming students, Jason believes.

"It's a way that they can at least touch the water and know it's not going to burn you," he says. "We could tell them, 'Hey, you know, we're all human beings and this is what you're going to hear. But hear it from other students that survived the first year 'holocaust' if you will, and you'll see it isn't that bad.' It was actually just quite the opposite."

"Jason was a year ahead of me already, so he had kind of got through the ropes," said Otis. "He was opening up and willing enough to pass that knowledge on to me and to a few other of my medical school classmates."

Jason didn't tell the new students that it would be an easy ride, but it was an achievable goal. "The courses are hard because you have to focus on this memorization, not because they are so scientifically esoteric," he emphasized in the meetings. "It's because there's just so much information and you have to really buckle down. You have to treat this like a full-time job. It doesn't matter if you're white, black, Asian, whatever your ethnicity or your culture is, you're going to get the same books, you're going to have the same teachers. Even the bodies in gross anatomy are going to be relatively similar, for that matter. You're going to have the same opportunities to excel in school. Typically, if you don't, it's because there are other things going on outside of school in your personal life or something like that."

For Otis and the other new students, Jason's words were encouraging but also a reminder to stay focused.

"It was huge because we were able to do fairly well in med school," said Otis. "I think a lot of that was due to his willingness to be open and just giving, in a sense, because a lot of times you don't see that in med schools. Medical schools are a very competitive environment. For some people it can be like, 'I want to do well and I don't want anybody else to do well.' And so for Jason to kind of reach back and give some helping hands to people and get some knowledge to them, it was huge for sure."

Jason's generosity in freely sharing his knowledge and his time is a character trait that comes up frequently when colleagues and friends talk about him. It's an attribute that would become even more apparent in his medical practice and his involvement with safety developments in motor sports.

"He's always kind of somebody like a big brother to me," was how Otis described the relationship that began at that meeting. "Having that big brother figure and how he was towards me, not just for my first year at med school, but even throughout my entire career, he's been giving of himself in multiple ways."

Jason is quick to point out that LSU already had a program in place to familiarize incoming students, including minorities, with expectations about medical school. For students like Otis, however, Jason's contribution was to bring the orientation to a personal, one-on-one basis.

Additionally, Jason's work ethic and his dedication to succeed were apparent to Otis. "I can recall a few times in medical school when I would see him and we would talk," said Otis. "You could just look at his face and tell he'd put in some serious time for studying, and I was like, 'Man, you look kinda beat. How long have you been awake?' And I recall him being up for, like, two days, literally 48 hours plus, getting ready for an exam. Even though he kind of looked a little beat, functionally he was totally normal."

Otis noted that this is a characteristic that is still evident in Jason's medical practice. "I think he's kind of built for being a neurosurgeon, because he can just turn on a switch and be in a focus mode for as long as he needs to," he said, adding that when Jason is out of that mode he can change his focus to something completely different such as working on his racing go-karts. "But it's amazing how he could turn that focus switch on and he could be locked in on something for hours at a time, for days at a time."

Jason's own training continued at the LSU School of Medicine. With the goal of becoming a surgeon, he was naturally anticipating getting inside the O.R. However, he says, "As a med student, for the first two years, you're in classes, then in your third year you would enter clinicals."

The term 'clinicals' refers to the period of education in which medical students become involved with patient care and get hands-on training in various domains of medicine.

CHAPTER 23

Hands-on in the O.R.

"I saw that you can change the lives of people in different ways and you don't necessarily even have to be in med school or be a doctor." – Jason Cormier

JASON CLEARLY RECALLS the first time he was officially 'hands-on' in the O.R. during his third year at med school. He was retracting – using a surgical instrument to separate the edges of a surgical incision.

"Now granted, I was doing that before I went to med school," Jason admits, referring to his time working in the O.R. in Baton Rouge, "So I couldn't wait to get in and do it! But the difference in doing it before school and now in med school is that now it really counts. Now it's not just this fantasy. Now I can break from the operating room and go put on my white coat, even though it was short, not the full lab coat. It was a short white coat because that's what medical students wear."

But it was more than just the white coat. "I could go see patients and officially say, 'Hey, I'm a student doctor and how are you doing?' I had a real part, essentially, in their care from the standpoint that I could truly learn about the medicines and all that and be focused on being trained to become a good doctor and not just a good employee of the hospital."

It was becoming increasingly obvious to Jason that he felt the need to have a positive effect on the people with whom he came into contact, whether or not it was as a doctor.

"It's weird in a way," he reveals, "I saw that you can change the lives of people in different ways and you don't necessarily even have to be in med school or be a doctor. I think just from the standpoint of transporting people to the operating room, helping out with prepping them in the operating room, I was enthusiastic. I was like, 'Man! This is what I wanna do!' But back then, it wasn't official, it was still a dream and a fantasy.

"And so now, in my third year at med school, it's like now I feel even more a part of this. This dream, this fantasy is really happening and please don't pinch me. I don't want to ever wake up!"

By his third year, Jason could feel the increased confidence and responsibility that he was achieving. "You could make suggestions and not feel like you're speaking out of turn," he points out. "And now you're reading and learning the backgrounds of all the information that until now you've really just been observing. Why are they doing this? Why are they doing that? And now I truly have a grasp of all the physiology that goes into it, the interconnections of the anatomy and what these people go through. Now I could ask those questions."

As he progressed through med school, Jason was certain that he would become a surgeon, and his chosen specialty was heart surgery. "I remember I was pursuing cardiovascular surgery," he says. "Cardio-thoracic surgeons. They were at the pinnacle of medicine and I was like, 'I'm just going for it all.' They were the crème de la crème of medicine at the time, or that's what I believed."

"In my third year in med school, I was doing all my research in heart surgery and back surgery and I helped develop an aortic loop measurement tool and one thing and another," he notes with a degree of modesty. "There were two heart surgeons, Dr Samuel Webb and Dr. Peter Mulder. Dr. Webb developed the perfusion machine and Dr. Mulder had a number of different things that he had developed, and I got to work with those guys."

Medical students were required to make presentations to the Board to show their proficiency. "It was basically, just walk in front of the Board and read from something," he says. But Jason decided that he was going to mount a full-court press and make a real impression. To achieve this, he called on some friends back in Baton Rouge.

"I did a full PowerPoint presentation," he says. "I was like, 'I'm going to do it!' Everything about the heart. I brought in knowledge. The people that I had worked with at Baton Rouge General Medical Center made this little kit for me, I had all the tools and the section things. I was the coolest person!" he says with a laugh. "My marks were really good!"

Jason became eligible to be a member of Alpha Omega Alpha (AOA) Honor Medical Society, and also the Aesculapian Society, an organization that functions as a liaison between students and faculty. "That was pretty cool," he says.

CHAPTER 24

Heart in the wrong place?

"If you really want to be challenged, Neurosurgery is the last true art of surgery, and you are only as good as your last complication." – Najeeb Thomas, MD

BUT JASON WAS BEGINNING to have doubts about his chosen field of thoracic and cardiovascular surgery.

"I figured that maybe I was chasing thoracic surgery for the wrong reasons," he says. "Because when I was at the hospital, cardiovascular surgeons, thoracic surgeons, they were like the top ones. I started thinking, 'Am I going at it because I really want thoracic surgery, or am I doing it because it's at the top and I'm going to prove I can do it?'"

However, he wasn't convinced that he should turn away from that path. He had invested so much of his time, his energy and his enthusiasm into pursuing that line of surgery. He was approaching the point where he would complete his four-year course at LSU and receive his MD degree. After completing medical school, he would be expected to enter a residency program, the postgraduate training in his chosen medical field.

"Literally, when I was trying to write my personal statement for residency, it took me days and days and days and I'm trying to think of these things," he recalls. "I kept tearing up the essay, like, 'This doesn't sound right, this doesn't sound right.' I'm saying to myself, 'Speak from your heart,' and I'm saying, 'I am. This is weird. Thoracic surgery. This is what I wanna do. I'm sure it's what I want to do." But it was getting harder to convince himself that he should continue to follow the path to thoracic surgery.

As Jason had said, he knew God was in his corner and maybe God nudged events just a little.

About that time, Jason was supposed to go in to do a rotation at Johns Hopkins Hospital in Baltimore, Maryland. The hospital shares a campus with the prestigious Johns Hopkins University School of Medicine. However, apparently there was a mix-up with the necessary paperwork.

"It was an 'away rotation' and just didn't work out," says Jason, "So I sat down and spoke to the counselors at LSU and they said, 'Well, you can take courses here instead,' because you're given three months where you can do kind of what you want to."

His counselors told him that he could take a rotation in either neurology or neurosurgery. He could go ahead and do that now and there was an opportunity that he could graduate from med school early. It didn't take Jason long to decide. "I thought, well, I know I want to be in the operating room," he says. "At least I know that, so I chose to do rotation in neurosurgery, and I said, 'Well okay! I'll just do that!'"

Jason is honest about the start of the neurosurgery rotation, regarding it as simply something he had to do to complete his med school training. "The first couple of days I didn't really care that much," he confesses. "I was not even really listening to the questions. This is just a formality to me. I'm thinking my grades are good, I was going to matriculate to a top-notch general surgery program and ultimately to thoracic surgery. I was going to be a heart surgeon."

However, one event happened to change that path forever.

"During the rotation, Dr. Klein had these tumor boards at journal clubs on Saturdays, and I attended one on the second week." Jason remembers what he would later see as a significant moment in his career. "Four residents got up and they presented the same brain tumor in four different patients, but the tumors were located in different sections of the brain. And they described how each patient woke up with a different complication, a different deficit. So that hit me like, Whoa! That's pretty cool, that's impressive."

He realized that neurosurgery could present fascinating challenges that were unique in that there was no such thing as a routine or predictable case when it came to brain surgery. Already troubled by thoughts about his original goal of becoming a heart surgeon, he could now see the intriguing opportunities offered by neurosurgery.

"I sat down and spoke to the head heart surgeon at Ochsner Hospital in Jefferson, Louisiana," says Jason. "A very nice guy; he spent 45 minutes with me. He said, 'Jason, I cannot in good faith tell you to go into heart surgery because I don't think you're going to like the monotony of it. You go in, you do a heart surgery, you are resecting, rerouting arteries, this that and the other. It's really changing a whole lot. They've come out with stents so now we're just getting patients that wake up, they're on ventilators for days and days. You're going to get bored with the monotony. I don't think that's what you want. You're just going into one sector. Now you can do peripheral stuff, but I don't think that's what you want to do.' I thought, 'Gosh, okay.'"

Jason also had a conversation with a well-known highly respected neurosurgeon, Dr. Najeeb Thomas. Jason recalls Dr. Thomas's words that day: "He said, 'Man, I think neurosurgery is the last true art of surgery.' He said this – and it sticks with me all the time – he said, 'If you really want to be challenged, Neurosurgery is the last true art of surgery, and you're only as good as your last complication.' I said, 'Wow, that's pretty heavy.'"

Those thoughts were still in Jason's mind the next day when he was involved in a procedure as part of his rotation. "It was a pituitary tumor and we went in through the nose," he says. "It brought back memories of surgery from Baton Rouge when I was a transporter because I would sneak around, I'd get in the rooms, and there was one guy, Dr. David Depp, who would see me hanging around the rooms. He was a vascular surgeon. He said, 'Are you interested in this?' I said, 'Yeah,' and he said, 'You want to scrub in?' I was like, What? You want me to scrub in?! I washed my hands. And after that, that was the greatest thing on earth. It was my utopian dream. I went home and called every friend I knew and I was like, I scrubbed in, I touched anatomy. They started bringing me into more and more operations, so that just solidified that, yes, medicine is where I'm going."

Now, in the O.R. assisting in the surgery on the pituitary tumor, that same feeling of exhilaration returned. He fully understood Dr Thomas's assertion that neurosurgery was the last true art of surgery. Jason had some serious decisions to make.

By a curious twist of fate, once again music played a significant role in Jason's destiny.

CHAPTER 25

Bring Me To Life

"I remember going to his dorm room in New Orleans med school. I opened the refrigerator to get a beer and I saw a human brain in there! And I was like, 'What the hell?'" –
Dallas Webb

"THIS IS WHERE MUSIC really came back into my life in a meaningful way," says Jason. "There was a song called 'Bring Me to Life' by Evanescence. In the chorus it says, 'Save me from the nothing I've become.' What that meant to me was I was pursuing thoracic surgery for the wrong reasons because I had become really interested in neuro."

The band Evanescence was co-founded by singer and pianist Amy Lee. Initially an indie rock group, their big break came when they were signed to a record deal that resulted in the album *Fallen.* The album has sold more than 17 million copies worldwide. "Bring Me to Life" was the debut single from the album and the song inspired millions of listeners in addition to Jason Cormier.

The lyrics of the Evanescence song brought into focus his concerns about a future in thoracic surgery compared to the thrill he was experiencing as he began to work in neurosurgery.

"I remembered all the cool things," he says, "People waking up from spinal surgery and saying, 'Oh my gosh, you saved me,' and then the tumor surgery, going through the nose; I thought

The lyrics of "Bring Me to Life" by Evanescence had a life-changing effect on Jason.

that was one of the coolest things on earth. One time I saw a guy who had tried to commit suicide with a crossbow. All these different things. And they lived." Because of the skill of a neurosurgeon.

Jason met up with his longtime friend Dallas Webb and described his experiences during his rotation and the inspiration he drew from the Evanescence song. "I just laid it on him. And he said, 'I've never heard you feel this way. I've never heard you this excited about something. Neurosurgery is what you should do.'"

That incident has remained lodged in Dallas' memory, partly because of what he found in Jason's fridge.

"I remember going to his dorm room in New Orleans med school," said Dallas. "I opened the refrigerator to get a beer and I saw a human brain in there! And I was like, 'What the hell?' And then he told me that it was actually a lifelike model of a brain! He'd take the skull apart piece by piece. He would take the replica brain out and take it apart then he'd put it all back together, over and over again. I was like, 'Man you really love that.' And Jason said, 'Yeah, I guess I do. You know what? I need a challenge in life and I think I can do this.'"

"That was the closer for me," says Jason. "After that I never turned back."

Previously, he had tried to write his essay as part of his application for residency in a general surgery program, which is the prerequisite for cardiothoracic fellowship, but the words just didn't seem to come to him. Now he was applying for a neurosurgical residency and the words flowed easily as he was writing from the heart.

Evanescence, who inspired Jason with their song 'Bring Me to Life,' would touch Jason's life again a few years later, as we shall see.

CHAPTER 26

Moving on to a residency

"I was actually praying the night before match day that Michigan would pass over me because it was so cold there!"
– Jason Cormier

JASON WENT ON TO a residency program at Duke University Medical Center in Durham, North Carolina. However, the selection process for a residency is almost as complex as the NFL Draft. "Ultimately, there's a 'match day' and you kind of have to be chosen," he says. "You choose them, they choose you as well, and the numbers have to match up.

"The medical facilities list their choice of students in order, one through ten and you list your choice of schools, one through ten in the order you would prefer to do your residency," Jason explained. "The school picked two residents a year. For instance, Duke I think, was number two on my list. Apparently, at the first choice on my list I was looked over and then the numbers matched up for Duke."

Jason admitted that at the time you have no idea what is going on. "Michigan was my first choice," he notes, "And I was actually praying the night before match day that Michigan would pass over me because it was so cold there! Then I started hearing that the training at Duke was better for what I needed. I was hearing things and I was like, 'Gosh, maybe I should have put Duke first.' So yeah, it just worked out perfectly the way I wanted it to."

In retrospect, considering just how much goes back and forth in the residency selection process, it worked out well for Jason. "If I were to have placed Duke as my number one choice but they had five other students ranked ahead of me, I probably would not have gone to Duke," he acknowledges.

Moving on from med school at LSU to his residency at Duke, Jason was able to focus on neurosurgery.

A surgical residency program is for doctors who have already attained a medical degree but are still in training to become qualified surgeons. Residencies last anywhere from five to eight years and are notorious for the long hours and strenuous work that surgical residents are required to undertake. Technically, in the first year, participants are referred to as 'interns' and are then deemed residents from their second year forward, working under the supervision of an attending surgeon.

As Jason had experienced at LSU, residents (initially as interns) rotate through different services to familiarize them with other specialized areas they might encounter in their practice.

In addition to surgery, residents are expected to handle other tasks such as prepping patients for surgery and completing physical examinations as well as practicing procedures in a skills lab. They are often required to do what most residents refer to as "scut work," non-medical assignments that can include putting in nurses' orders, accompanying patients to procedures, talking to patients or their families and obtaining signatures on medical consent forms. Residents receive a salary but at a considerably lower rate than fully accredited surgeons.

The long hours and intense responsibilities mean that many who enter a residency program never complete it. For Jason, dropping out was never going to be an option.

Duke was working out well for Jason in his intern year in residency. But once again, family matters became a determining factor in the progression of Jason's medical education. While he was still at med school at LSU, his mother had been diagnosed with unstable angina and underwent heart surgery; she continued to have heart problems afterwards. While Jason was at Duke, his sister Dolores was diagnosed with cancer and began to undergo treatment.

Duke University Medical Center is in Durham, North Carolina, 964 miles from Lafayette, Louisiana. Jason was becoming increasingly aware of that distance and the time it would take him to get home in an emergency.

"With my mother still being sick and my sister's cancer diagnosis, it became one of those things where I started looking for a program that was really closer to home if something were to happen," he says.

As he researched suitable residency programs within a reasonable driving distance of Lafayette, The University of Alabama at Birmingham (UAB) rose to the top of the list.

CHAPTER 27

Leaving Duke for UAB

"I was like, 'Oh my God! You made it! You made it!' You know, I was so touched by that." – Dolores Cormier-Zenon

"I WASN'T UPSET or unhappy at Duke," Jason stipulates, "But I found that in the current situation with my family and also with the caliber of the things that they were doing at UAB from a clinical aspect that it was going to be the best thing for my career and for my own peace of mind to transfer to UAB. To get on a flight quickly from Durham would be much more difficult than getting on a flight or driving home from UAB if something were to happen." Dr Friedman, the chairman of Duke Neurosurgery at the time, was always kind and understanding, as were my fellow residents.

And at the same time, Jason knew that he would be getting-top notch training. There were a number of surgeons around the country that Jason would have liked to train with, but he was particularly excited about the opportunity to train under Dr. Mark Hadley at UAB.

When that opportunity arose, Jason says, "It was just tough to beat it. I took the chance and it was difficult because I had a number of friends that I'd made at Duke and they didn't want me to leave at all. I'd actually purchased a piece of property and so that was an issue."

However, Jason quickly realized it was the right move, particularly when he met with Dr. Hadley.

"We got Jason Cormier in transfer from Duke where he had first started his neurosurgical career," said Dr. Hadley. "I was the Program Director in charge of all the residents and resident training. I liked him and it wasn't just me that agreed to take him on. We rarely take someone in who wants to transfer from another program, but Cormier was a solid guy."

Asked what impressed him about Jason, Dr. Hadley explained, "He's an accomplished guy and he exerts a personal presence of humility but also of competence, and yeah, I liked all those things. He's always been an athlete and an engaging guy. He participated in neurosurgical investigation and research when he was here so he did all the things that a resident must do in our program to graduate. He was a very good student, a very good resident. And, of course, he became a very good surgeon."

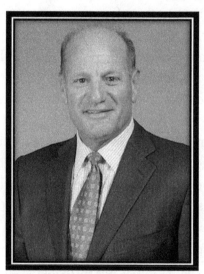

Mark N. Hadley, M.D., Professor of Neurosurgery at UAB.

Jason is well aware of how important that relationship was, and still is. "It turned out to be a really good thing," he says. "Dr. Hadley took me under his wing and he pretty much gave me the keys, from the standpoint of teaching me his nuances of spinal surgery. That really jump-started my education and my confidence in spinal surgery."

For Jason, Dr. Hadley was more than a teacher, a mentor and a highly skilled surgeon.

"We just had really deep conversations, like kind of father and son, because I really didn't have a father after our dad just took off," says Jason. "Dr. Hadley would tell me things like, 'Everyone gets judged and they're going to judge you differently than they judge me. You have it in you. You are a born surgeon.'"

During those private conversations, Dr. Hadley would frequently tell Jason, "I want you to be better than me." It almost became a mantra that Jason always tried to live up to.

"I remember whenever he said that, I was kind of overwhelmed by the comment," recalls Jason, "Because I was like, 'Wow man! You're super-accomplished. There's no way in the world!' I respected him to no end because he had just an amazing surgical acumen. He was a quick thinker. He could fight his way out of any sort of issue intraoperatively. And some of those things, you can't really teach. He used to tell me that, 'You're an athlete and in the same way you are born with things that are going to start to come to you.' I didn't understand that until finally I was up against some of those challenges and I was able to find my way out thankfully through his guidance and mentorship."

Dr. Hadley pulled no punches when he talked to Jason about what to expect going forward. He knew that Jason had not had the same opportunities or background as most people who were entering this profession.

"I counseled him about this as fatherly advice about going to Lafayette," said Dr Hadley bluntly. "I said, 'People may misconstrue you and you're going to have to battle that and have thick skin. But maintain your equanimity and your composure and your excellence and people – not all, but many – will forget what color you are. They won't come up and hug you around the neck and kiss you on the side of the neck like I do often. But they'll forget when they realize you're just really a great person. I'm sorry that you are going to have to prove that to some people instead of people taking it at face value like they might for someone else. But that's unfortunately the circumstance."

Having become virtually a member of the Hadley family, Jason had visited the family home on many occasions while at UAB. "I'd probably been to his house more times than any of the other residents," he recalls, "And one evening we had journal club over there. It was weird; I was basically showing some of the other Attendings there how to get into the house, and they were just dumbfounded, like, 'How do you know how to get in and how do you know where the door is?'" He laughs now at the memory. "I thought to myself: 'Well, you know, I come here! This is like home.'"

As his residency progressed, Jason spent more time in the O.R. with Dr. Hadley. "He just really became a true father and mentor," recalls Jason about those times. "Even in the operating room, there was always one or two of us who were assisting him. He would say his favorite saying, which was, 'Help dad out.' Or if something happened in the operating room when he would lose his temper and start firing off; we were the boys. He was like a coach in the operating room and so we could easily take it. It wasn't really a big deal because it was like my coach or my dad getting on me to do something, so I took it as just a corrective measure. And so yeah, we have a really great relationship today, and I call him often for advice."

Jason's decision to move his residency to UAB – to be closer to his hometown – proved to be the right one when his sister Dolores required surgery for her cancer.

As noted before, residents are on-call for many hours at a time, often in stressful circumstances, and a chance to sleep is often the only thing on their minds when they can finally stand down. Jason knew that Dolores' surgery had been scheduled in Lafayette while he was in Birmingham.

"I was on call when she had surgery," he says. "I had been on call all night, but I decided I was going to drive in anyway. And that was after 24 hours or 30 hours of being on call. I was there in the room with her husband Chris when she awakened from surgery."

It's a special moment that still means so much to Dolores. "When I went into surgery, he wasn't there because he was still at work," she recalled. "But when I woke up he was in the Recovery room beside me, so I woke up to see him. I was like, 'Oh my God! You made it! You made it!' You know, I was so touched by that. And after all the chemo finished and I had my surgery he was in the room, sitting in the chair reading a newspaper after driving all night. I was so touched."

Jason knew that his family was aware of the rigors he was going through and understood the grueling hours that residents have to work as they complete their training.

"Dolores wouldn't have been hurt if I would not have been able to make it," says Jason. "She would have been very understanding and just written it off like, 'I know that he's very busy and I know that I'm in his prayers, but he just couldn't make it because he was working.' She wasn't necessarily expecting me to show up. It would have been a phone call and that would have sufficed so it was kind of over-the-top. She was overwhelmed when I decided, Yeah, I'm on call but I'm gonna drive there after I get off and just head down to Louisiana."

Remembering the surprise and the comforting presence of her brother at that moment, Dolores said, "I still tear-up now, about what he did just for me. Just because he wanted to make sure I'd have another chance at life, you know?"

In the weeks following Dolores' surgery, Jason kept an eye on his sister's progress while he completed his residency in Alabama.

"Her doctors would keep me informed on the latest data and the pros and cons of what they expected from an operative standpoint," says Jason, adding, "But it was frustrating, the fact that you're going to be missing things that you really want to be close to."

CHAPTER 28

The Chief Resident

"You are expected to know everything. It's on your shoulders." – Jason Cormier

AS JASON'S RESIDENCY AT UAB progressed, he took on more responsibilities as Chief Resident.

"When you're the Chief, you're responsible for all the residents," says Jason, describing the position. "You're responsible for assigning them to surgery. You're responsible for sometimes didactic lectures and arranging cadaveric labs, etcetera. So you're at the helm of all the residents, basically. You take all the phone calls that come in from outside hospitals asking for patients to be transferred in. You are on call almost every night when the in-house resident under you is calling and giving you a scenario. You review the films and you ultimately make the decision to call the Attending to come in, so they treat you like you are an Attending. It's part of what they call transitional training."

An 'Attending' is a medical doctor who is responsible for the overall care of a patient in a hospital who may also supervise and teach medical students, interns and residents involved in the patient's care.

"As a Chief, you are expected to know everything," says Jason. "It's like this is your trial before you get out and practice on your own. It's intimidating for the first few weeks of taking Chief Call. It's on your shoulders."

Adding to the pressure, Chief Call would normally be undertaken during a resident's final year. However, Jason and one other resident started Chief coverage in their second-to-last year. Jason saw it as a sign of the confidence that both Dr. Hadley and Dr James Markert , chairman of UAB Neurosurgery, had in his capabilities.

"It's the confirmation and last step if you will, to see if you are ready to go to the next level and graduate from the program," says Jason. "There are a lot of people that don't ever make it to the Chief year. They get released first and there are some people that don't make it past the Chief year."

It was a challenging assignment, but Jason could see the benefits that he gained from his early assignment as Chief. He reflects on it this way: "I'll tell you the good thing about it is, with the experiences that we had, we were ready long before we even started our last year. We were taking Chief Call, and in our fifth year, we would go to Children's Hospital to cover the pediatric service as well as the V.A. Hospital. This is something that they immersed you in relatively quickly if they trusted you."

In addition to refining their skills as surgeons, residents need to learn what it takes to operate their own business, if they intend to go into private practice when they graduate from the program. This is where the other side of 'transition training' comes in.

"You have to be able to run a business," says Jason. "It's a very difficult thing to do because you're primarily focused on medicine. We used to have this saying at UAB: 'There are two reasons you're in a residency. One is to become a well-trained neurosurgeon, and the other is survival.' It really comes down to the survival of the fittest. It's tough. I mean, all the hours you work. You have to really remain coherent and understand what you're doing and you are constantly getting quizzed. It's how to live a segment of your life. In the end, the attending surgeons care about you and so they are both teaching and monitoring you in many different ways. I have so many people to thank at UAB, including the Attendings for their patience and trust, the fellow residents, nurse practitioners and physician assistants, nurses, scrub-techs, aides, secretaries, in addition to my friends outside the hospital who made Birmingham my home, still today," says Jason

CHAPTER 29

Returning home to practice

"'You weren't as accurate as you could be,' – this was here in front of these other people – 'about Cormier and his candidacy and his person.'" – Mark Hadley, MD

WITH HIS EXCELLENT CREDENTIALS and the 'trial by fire' experience of being a Chief Resident at UAB, Jason was more than ready to set up his practice as a neurosurgeon. He began exploring his options during his final year at UAB and was already being approached by neurological healthcare facilities.

"I had offers from many different cities and they even still come in today," he recalls. In fact, he still receives up to three or four emails a day for opportunities in other locations.

One weekend at UAB, he was heading back to Lafayette for a visit with his family and told his friend Dr. Dani Bidros of his travel plans. "Dani said, 'Hey, look up Alan Appley when you get there,' and I said, 'Okay.'"

Dr. Alan Appley was in practice at Acadiana Neurosurgery in Lafayette. "I got an interview with Dr. Appley and I really didn't know anything about him at that time," says Jason frankly. "I felt, well, my initial interview there will be a nice trip to go and say hello and visit and have a nice meal at home. So when I met with Dr. Appley he said, 'This could be a place for you to really set up. Your roots are here and you can really make something special here, coming back as a neurosurgeon.' I said, 'Well, I'm looking for a bigger town. I think I'm going to outgrow this town pretty soon once I get here.'" However, Jason felt that Dr. Appley had a really good personality and the meeting went well.

Apparently, that feeling was mutual. "He was in town interviewing for another position and we got in touch when he was here that weekend," noted Dr. Appley. "We met and hit it off and clearly, we were on the same page neurosurgically and I knew he was well trained."

Jason also considered some other options in Lafayette. "I interviewed with three different hospitals here and one of the hospitals was completely out of the ballpark just in terms of what they were offering in the way of the contract," he says. "The other two were pretty attractive contracts but they had some language in there that I really didn't agree with. More than anything, they were restrictive in terms of what I could do joining surgery centers and whatnot."

After the round of interviews in Lafayette, Jason returned to Birmingham. A few weeks earlier, he had interviewed for a position in Georgia and the prospects had looked good. Now back at UAB, Jason reviewed their offer.

"At that point, I actually signed a contract with the group in Georgia, located about twenty minutes outside of downtown Atlanta," he says. "They wanted me to be the director of their neuroscience and neurosurgery program and things were going well. The hospital signed the contract and they were on board, but it just kind of fell apart for whatever reason."

He believes that the attorney for the practice seemed to be dragging out the process unnecessarily.

It was particularly frustrating for Jason, as he says: "I had started looking early on in my last year at UAB because I didn't want to get caught with three months left to graduate and then, here we go, I'm looking for a practice. But then with the process in Georgia dragging on and on, that's exactly what happened."

With the end of his residency at UAB rapidly approaching, he decided to drop the Georgia option. Going into practice in Lafayette was looking increasingly attractive. He was feeling drawn back there, he says. "It was home but first and foremost my sister was sick at the time, battling breast cancer, and in addition to that, my mother was here and she had some illnesses. It just made sense that I should at least consider coming home."

He wasn't sure if that opportunity at Acadiana Neurosurgery still existed. Once again, it seemed that Fate was going to step in and move things along.

"I thought, maybe I should revisit the situation with Dr. Appley but I'm not really sure what I'm going to do about it," he says. "Before I reached out to him, I received a text message. I think it was like 12:30 or one o'clock in the morning and I thought it was a spine rep asking me a question or something and I was really about to, you know, give it to him! 'Why have you texted me that late at night?' People knew it wasn't uncommon for me to be awake at weird hours. I'm always awake but for someone from the industry to just up and do it; I didn't know who they were and that was the problem."

It was unusual for Jason to respond to a text from an unrecognized text number, particularly in the early hours of the morning.

"I don't know why but – for some reason, to just entertain the conversation and try to draw out who this really was so I could properly address them and their company – I answered the text. It turns out it was Dr. Appley and I was like, well, first of all it's a good thing I didn't say something negative! And secondly, he keeps my hours so that was already the start of a symbiotic situation. We had more conversations and then when I looked at their contract, after speaking to him – because he really championed getting me there – he got them to remove the restrictive language and he was going to make space for me in his practice."

"I think he could see that he would have a better future and have a little 'mentor opportunity' by coming to work with me," said Dr. Appley. "I was in solo practice at the time and I happened to have space in the office. I had just built an office actually and everything just kind of fell into place. We needed new blood in town and I could use the help and he needed a good opportunity to work with somebody."

Jason says that, at that point, "I really didn't have a reason to say no. All the pillars aligned, if you will, and I thought, 'I guess this is where I'm going to start my practice.' I was excited about it because of my sister and my mother, etcetera, but they had removed the restrictive language and I felt, okay, this is a sign, and that's how I ended up coming back home."

Although all the neurosurgeons in Lafayette are in their own private practice, they belong to an alliance called Neurological Associates of Louisiana and that is an organization that handles duties such as office payroll, billing, insurance policies, and so on. This means that instead of being a practice of perhaps four people, they are represented under an umbrella of, say, fifty employees.

Jason recalls that there was something of a vetting process regarding his proposed plans to practice in Lafayette. "All the neurosurgeons would meet and they would have a discussion," he explains. "They would ask, 'Are we okay bringing this guy here because this is our playground and we don't want to bring somebody in here that's not very competent or it's going to make Lafayette look bad.' It's basically a round table discussion and it might be, 'Okay I agree,' and maybe there might be someone that says 'No, I don't really like the guy, I heard this or that.' It's the time to share ideas and information that you have for or against that person planning to come here."

As part of their research, the group reached out to Dr. Mark Hadley, the Program Director at UAB. "When Jason was applying for a position at Lafayette, I told those guys that this was a well-trained resident, a very bright resident, a very capable resident and remarkable individual and one that I fully endorsed," explained Dr. Hadley. "And of course, I tell them all about his scores, which are well above average, and his participation and things of that nature. That was my endorsement, about his personal integrity and so on, and I wrote it in the letter I sent them."

"I knew he came from a good program," noted Dr. Appley. "Just in talking to him we hit it off in terms of our philosophy and taking care of patients. I had a good feeling in terms of his character and his training. Those were the most important factors."

In August of 2010, Jason began his practice at Acadiana Neurosurgery in Lafayette, Louisiana and quickly began to build his reputation as a surgeon. He admits that, at first, being in practice as a surgeon could be scary because, as he says, "In residency you had someone watching over you. If you were coming to a point where you weren't sure about something or there was a mistake that might be made, there was someone that you could reach out to and ultimately you were under their supervision. Whereas now starting out at Acadiana Neurosurgery I was basically an equal partner in that situation. I was not working for Dr. Appley. We essentially had our own practices under the umbrella of Acadiana Neurosurgery. It was a different world because now the buck stops with you. Anything happens, they're going to name you, not UAB."

However, that wasn't a deterrent. "I was good with it," he says. "I was ready."

When he started out, he was often performing microdiscectomies, minimally invasive surgical procedures performed on patients with a herniated lumbar disc. During this surgery, a surgeon removes portions of the herniated disc to relieve pressure on the spinal nerve column. "These are pretty straightforward cases," notes Jason, "And I remember doing cervical fusions with

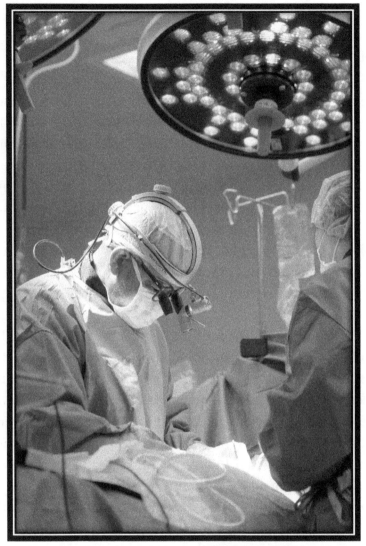

Dr. Cormier in surgery. Neurosurgery and spinal surgery require extraordinary precision.

Dr. Appley and it got to the point where I felt as if I'm just wasting his time. It was more of a weaning process to get me away from needing that other person looking over my shoulder. Is this right? Is that right? Because now I'm on my own."

Looking back, he recognizes that pivotal moment: "I think when I did my first aneurysm case, that's when it was all pretty well solid. I was confident at that point, essentially."

That was apparent to Dr. Appley as well. "I could tell that he was extremely skilled," he said, "Even just out of residency, he was skilled at vascular neurosurgery, cerebrovascular, which included vascular abnormalities of the brain like aneurysms, vascular malformations and tumors. That was very impressive as all of these procedures are extremely complex. I have seen him perform surgeries that many academic institutions would not deal with and have great success. I was very impressed with his skillset as it was clear that he was one of a kind, extremely talented, while at the same time he remained open to my criticisms. My wife and I called him "The Key Master," his hands are simply that good.

Three years after Jason began his practice in Lafayette, Dr. Hadley was in Denver attending an executive meeting of the Academy of Neurological Surgery. "I had just stepped out of the meeting and I'm with these other chairmen and leaders, maybe five guys, all very famous neurosurgeons," he recalled. "We're just in the middle of a lobby area. A gentleman walks up to me and says, 'Dr. Hadley?' And I said 'Yes.' And he says, 'I'm Dr. Steve Goldware and I'm one of the partners of the group that hired Jason Cormier.' I said, 'Oh yes, it's great to see you.' And he said, 'Well, you know you talked to us and sent us a letter about Jason Cormier and that's part of the reason we hired him. But you weren't very accurate, you weren't as accurate as you could be,' – this was here in front of these other people – 'about Cormier and his candidacy and his person.'"

Dr. Hadley was momentarily speechless, aware that the surgeons involved with Neurological Associates of Louisiana "were all white guys," as he put it. "And I think, 'My God!' and kind of take a step back," he said. "The guys I'm with, they're looking at me like, holy shit, what did Hadley do here? And then Dr. Goldware said, 'I just want you to know this guy is even better than you said. He has made an unbelievable contribution to the practice, to our community and our personal lives. I consider this young man to be one of the most remarkable men I've ever met, and I want to thank you, sir.'"

Mark Hadley's emotions at that moment were a mixture of relief, pride and exhilaration. "How about that! How does that make you feel! You know, that kind of thing? I'm thinking it's going in the other direction. I was going to be stunned if it was something negative but still… I didn't tell the group in Lafayette that we treat Jason like he's my son or 'he's a member of our family' kind of thing, but you know it was that kind of endorsement. It makes me cry because I love the kid! I just love him as a man and I'm so proud of him."

CHAPTER 30

God doesn't want this to happen

"I thought, 'Well, this can't be the same person. This is definitely not the same person.' I said, 'Okay, hang on one second.'" – Jason Cormier

AS A NEUROSURGEON, Jason deals with life-changing – even life-saving – events every day, most of which arise unpredictably. Many of the events that Jason remembers most vividly involve children and teenagers because they are the ones who are just starting on Life's journey when a serious brain injury or affliction threatens to bring them down.

Jason tells the story of one particular incident that affected him deeply.

"There was this kid who was around eighteen years old," he recalls. "He'd gone out one night and I think he had gotten really badly beaten up. When he came into the hospital there was blood all over his head to the point where his friends didn't know what to do. They dropped him off and just left him in the E.R. because they didn't want to get in trouble.

"I got to the E.R. and they consulted me. It was a really bad, horrible-looking CT Scan. Literally, after looking at the CT Scan, the brain scan, I was walking into the room to tell his mother, 'You know this is bad. From what the physicians are telling me, this is not good at all. He doesn't have any function.'

"Naturally, she was very upset. She was sobbing and she was

saying, 'God doesn't want this to happen. I'm praying for a miracle.' And I said, 'I can take this blood clot, but you know your son is not really going to do well with this. He could be in a vegetative state, or at least that's what the data suggests, and he doesn't have any function right now.' She continued to cry and was distraught. I said, 'Well, let me examine him myself and if there's anything which could be a guideline, I'll take him to surgery.'

"I examined him and I mean he was in really bad shape. It was one of those things that you know is not going to turn out well, but he had just some movement reacting to pain which is something.

"I knew he was just eighteen or so and that's the main reason, essentially, to take him but the outcome was pretty much determined that it wasn't going to turn out well at all. But I decided to take him to surgery, and I performed a craniotomy and a frontal lobectomy. I removed part of the frontal lobe of his brain that had been damaged by severe trauma.

"The father came in the next day and I told him and the boy's mother all that happened postoperatively. I said, 'This is bad. I took him but I'm very worried that this is not going to turn out well.' I just wanted to prepare them.

"On day number two, not much changed and at this point I'm getting pressure from the critical care service. They were saying, 'What are we going to do? Should we start talking about withdrawal of care,' and so on. I could understand their position as he's really not doing anything. We had ruled out seizures and everything.

"On day number three, I was expecting to come in and talk to the family and say, 'We've given this three days. He's not doing well and they want to remove the breathing tube. He's really just not functioning.' I started to walk into the room in the ICU and his breathing tube was out. He was actually eating a hamburger and he looked at me and said, 'What's up?'

"I thought, 'Well, this can't be the same person. This is definitely not the same person.' And so I said, 'Okay, hang on one second.' I stepped out and called the nurse. I looked at my patient log and he was still registered to this room. I said, 'Where's my craniotomy patient?' I was thinking that this is not the person and she says, 'No, that's your patient.' I said, 'Okay. The craniotomy I did three days ago? That patient?' And she says, 'Yes, sir.'

"I said, 'Well, this is one to remember! This is crazy!' I'm still in disbelief. I walk in there and sure enough, I mean it's him, and he's talking. He's not all there but he's eating, he's functional, and he's moving everything. He doesn't know where he is or the year, but he's functional. He knows his name, but he doesn't know what happened to him.

"Three months later, they came in for their follow-up appointment after he had gone to rehab. He said, 'Doc, I just want to say thank you for everything you've done.' And I said, 'Man, don't thank me. Thank your mother. I was not going to operate on you. This is your mother's doing.'

"It made me realize that mothers always fight for their kids. It just kind of reinstated that mothers know many times, even more than we do as physicians, and I don't know what it was but I'm glad I allowed her to drive me to do that. Because of that, the kid lived. He's got a job and he's working now.

"Something like that, it really affects you," he adds.

When patients are brought in with serious head injuries, it can be a chaotic scene with panic-stricken family members, hysterical with fear, surrounding the patient. Jason remembers just such a situation when a ten-year-old boy was brought in after being hit by a car. His parents were anxiously asking Jason what could be done. "I also had police officers there, asking me what to do and what his diagnosis was," says Jason who knew he had to be the voice of calm amidst the confusion. He quietly told them, "Just let me get to the patient."

Jason took him to surgery immediately. "He had a very large subdural hematoma, which occurs when a blood vessel near the surface of the brain bursts," says Jason. A subdural hematoma can be a life-threatening problem depending on the size of the hematoma and the age of the patient because it can compress the brain. Older patients are less likely to require surgery as the hematomas, depending on the size and age of the patient will liquify and those patients will either avoid surgery or have a minimally invasive surgery later down the line.The surgery was complex but successful and Jason was able to remove the hematoma. A few years later, Jason received a letter in the mail from that former patient.

"When the kid had come in, there was a very poor prognosis of what was going to happen," says Jason. "And now he actually wrote a letter to me. He graduated valedictorian of his class when he was seventeen."

Hearing, years later, of lives that were not only saved but were successful and fulfilling is what makes Jason know that his choice to specialize in neurosurgery was the right path for him.

"It's a field that surely has its highs and lows and it's challenging," he admits. "There are some tragedies but there are many more good stories, I will say."

CHAPTER 31

The compassionate side

"I love the way he cares, his tremendous passion for his craft, whether it be playing basketball, whether it would be motorsports, whether it be the concussion work, whatever. You know, whatever he does, he does 120%." – John Picou

THERE IS ONE FACET of Jason's character that becomes apparent when listening to his fellow doctors, his colleagues, his patients and their family members. In addition to his skill as a surgeon, he demonstrates something equally important: a deep sense of compassion and caring for his patients.

John Picou has been Jason's friend since childhood. "We went into battle together," is how he describes their time on the basketball court. John went on to play pro basketball and then work for Dr. Shaquille O'Neal for four years before entering the business world. "Jason was always the first one to practice and always the last one to leave," John noted. "He is definitely inspirational to me. He's a leader by example. Talk is cheap. You can always talk about it but when you actually physically do it, you know, that's what really matters. He didn't talk about it much, but he showed it and led by example which was extremely impressive to me."

However, there is a side to Jason that made an even deeper – and more personal – impression on John. "My godfather, my Uncle Brett, who was like a father and a mentor to me, was diagnosed with a rare brain cancer," said John. "When I found out about it, the first person I reached out to was Dr. Cormier."

Apparently, John's Uncle Brett had already seen another doctor who considered the tumor to be inoperable and recommended radiation and chemo treatments. John called Jason to tell him the worrying news.

"And Jason, being the man that he is, invited myself, my aunt and uncle to his house," said John. "We went over to his home, not his office, and he looked at the images and Jason talked to him and immediately got him into surgery. He created an additional year and a half of a beautiful life that he was able to experience with this brain tumor that he had, which was of all brain cancers, only 5% get this very rare tumor in their head. Jason was able to give him a quality life with his children, with his family, and I'll never forget it. It's just another testament to his morals and values as a man that he is and what he did. Yes, that's his craft and that's what he does, but he went above and beyond."

Jason's compassion extended beyond the eventual passing of his patient. "Even after my uncle passed away, my aunt had to finalize paperwork after the funeral and she drove to Lafayette," John recalled. "She walked in and Jason saw the look on her face. He looked at his staff and called my Aunt Paulette in and basically cleared his schedule for the entire day. That meant the world to her and gave her some positive closure, and people don't do that. Surgeons don't do that. They just don't.

"For him to do that speaks volumes about the man he is, his values and how much he truly cares about his patients. Afterwards, my aunt called me crying and just said how much it meant to her and how much she appreciated everything that Jason did for Uncle Brett."

John believes that the way Jason treats his patients as more than simply bodies on an O.R. table is an insight into his compassionate nature.

"I just love that about Jason," he said. "I love the way he cares, his tremendous passion for his craft, whether it be playing basketball, whether it would be motorsports, whether it be the concussion work, whatever. You know, whatever he does, he does 120%. And yes, he did it with nothing but his heart and his desire and his soul. He inspires me on a day-to-day basis."

Brain and spinal injuries are often the result of accidents. Because accidents often involve lawsuits, it's not unusual for doctors and lawyers to be involved in some of the same cases.

Grady Abraham is a practicing attorney in Lafayette, Louisiana, and handles personal injury cases. He says, "I deal with a lot of orthopedic surgeons, a lot of neurosurgeons because many of my clients are in need of serious, significant surgeries at some point. So there's a natural coming together between particular doctors and myself based on my practice and based on what they do."

Grady noted that in his practice he has dealt with doctors from all over Louisiana and other states. "I've never had any doctor get the results – and I mean long term results – that Jason has obtained for a lot of these people who are suffering," he stated unequivocally.

Jason's surgical skills and his remarkable work ethic are apparent to Grady and his clients. "The results he receives from all these surgeries, that's what's amazing," he said. But like many others who have observed Jason at work, it is his compassion that is as notable as his technical skill.

"He's excellent at what he does, and he cares." Grady emphasized that critical point. "He cares about the patients and that's a huge aspect. You've got to understand that many surgeons have the skill but they don't have the hands. Many have the hands but don't have the skill. Some have both of those two things but don't really care about the patients. They care about a paycheck. Jason is just complete in all of those areas, including caring about the patients. That is what makes him special."

Grady has seen how Jason's attitude has inspired hope and confidence in his patients. "He might be a little authoritative when it comes to staff because he demands excellence with his people," he allowed, "But when it comes to speaking to a patient who is scared, who doesn't understand what's going on, his bed-side manner, his ability to explain to people and give them the best health care they could possibly get anywhere in the world, it's something that's just done on a daily basis with him."

Grady noted that another component to a successful person who has the total package is just plain common sense. "A lot of times you have people that have this tremendous amount of in-tellect except they have no common sense," he remarked. "But Jason has that also. You can talk to him like a regular person. He can talk on any level and feel comfortable doing so."

It was also a characteristic noted by Jason's UAB mentor, Dr. Mark Hadley: "Jason is someone who is very compassionate, who's kind, smart and thoughtful, and has common sense – which is unusual in the male gender – and who is very accom-plished."

Dr. Mohamad ('Mo') Allam is a thoracic surgeon affiliated with multiple hospitals in Louisiana. He has had a unique oppor-tunity to work with Jason in the O.R. particularly on cases involving spinal surgery. It might seem intuitive that spinal sur-gery would be carried out from the patient's back but that is not always the case.

As Mo explained, "There are a lot of cases that I have to do with him approaching the spine from the front, from the belly all the way to the back of the spine. In situations like this, I am what's known as an 'exposure' surgeon. I can get him to see the spine so that he can do the surgery. We've done hundreds of cases together."

When approaching the spine from the front, a thoracic or cardiovascular surgeon is often involved. "It's a common term, with spinal surgery, to say, 'Who's doing your exposure?'" Mo added.

It might sound a bit gruesome to anyone unfamiliar with surgery, but it is necessary to have the internal organs moved aside so the spine is 'exposed' for the surgeon to work on. "Actually, there's a sac containing the bowels. You push the sac to the side, you push the vessels to the side. So basically, he's going to be straight-forward looking at bone and discs. Everything else is gone. It's out of the way."

Mo explained that the human body is made up of layers and, with this type of surgery, everything has to be moved layer by layer.

"Whenever we're doing those massive cases, he's very meticulous," said Mo, but there is more to it than that. "He's extremely easy to work with. He can work in situations that others could not work in. He is very capable of understanding the limitations of what I can expose."

Sometimes, with a very large patient, Mo is only able to expose about 70% of what Jason would really like to be able to see. Mo's observation about situations like this says a lot about Jason's character and the way he works with members of his team.

"The thing about Jason is that he understands that this is as much as I could give him," said Mo. "He's not going to whine about it like some others. He's going to deal with it. He's going to just work with what he has, which is very commendable for a neurosurgeon."

Mo gave an example of how Jason can inspire confidence in those he works with. "Jason might say to me, 'Mo, Here's the situation. What do you think? Can you get me two or three levels here?'

And I might say, 'Maybe. I'm not sure I'll be able to give them all to you,' and Jason, invariably, will say, 'Oh, you got that!'"

Jason shows the people he works with that he trusts them and they have his full confidence which in turn inspires them to do their very best. "He's very much on the positive side," said Mo, "Like, 'Oh yeah, you got this!' I think this is what he is all about. He is just a very trusting, extremely capable surgeon that does really very difficult cases."

CHAPTER 32

We're going to win this game

> "Under pressure we don't rise to the level of our expectations. We fall to the level of our training." – Archilochus (c. 680-645 BC)

DR. STEVE REES IS Vice President of Medical Affairs at Lafayette General Hospital and also runs the inpatient rehabilitation unit. He was the JV coach at St. Thomas More High School and assisted Coach Danny Broussard when Jason was on the team. "That's what I did before I went to medical school," said Steve. "Something that we have done through the years is play basketball together and so he'll come out and we have pick-up games and play. I have watched him for a long time."

Steve has observed that the determination that Jason showed on the basketball court in high school has continued to serve him in his chosen career. "To be able to go through medical school – which I can tell you, there are a lot of easier paths to go down – and then do another seven years after that, because that is how long a neurosurgical fellowship is," he pointed out. "To not only go to medical school but to end up being in the top 5% of the class and then deciding to go into neurosurgery, knowing that, when you get out, neurosurgery is not an easy job".

Steve then asked a rhetorical question. "Why do the smartest people pick the dumbest job?" By that, he means the most demanding and time-consuming calling in medicine. "I have always wondered that. Neurosurgeons work all the time. I'm always getting notes from them, at like three in the morning and stuff like that. And I'm like, man! If you are a neurosurgeon and you get called in the middle of the night for a trauma – I mean we are a trauma center at Lafayette General – you have to be there within thirty minutes. I deal with the rehabilitation and run the inpatient, so I deal with things on a much calmer, less urgent basis. But on trauma, they're going, 'Okay, we've got to do this now. And this is life or death, or this is going to determine whether you may or may not end up as a quadriplegic.'"

Steve paused, thinking of the pressure that neurosurgeons are under. "God bless them – you know they're doing God's work and they are saving lives and saving function," he said. "But, man! That's a dedicated, rough road that they have to go down. And Jason is like that.

"There has never been a time where I have called Jason and he has told me no, if he was available, even when he's not on call. I remember one time when he said, 'Well look, I'm out of town but I'll be back Sunday at noon. Tell them that Sunday at noon and I will take everything from there.' So I mean, that shows his dedication."

Dr. Steve Rees thought back to his days as high school Coach Rees. "I think that sort of thing comes from teamwork in playing ball, because you realize everybody has to be part of the team. And there are times when you're not going to be the starter or the star, but you're going to be the guy that comes in and has to do this special function when called. And there's other times when you are going to be the star."

Jason firmly believes that faultless, well-practiced teamwork is a key factor in successful surgery.

"There are times in the operating room when we are struggling and struggling and can't get things right," he says. "I'll take a deep

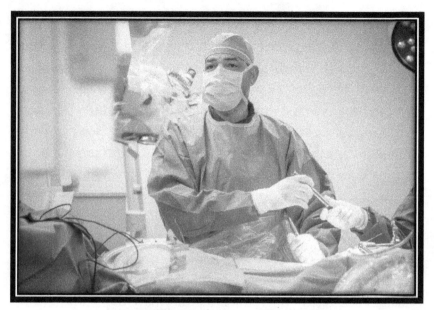

Dr. Jason Cormier begins another surgery.

breath. I'll look around the room and I tell everyone in there, 'We're going to win this game.' I try to keep the group inspired all the time. I remind them that it's teamwork. I tell my patients all the time that it's teamwork. You can't do this by yourself."

Teamwork in sports is important but in surgery it is literally vital: a matter of life and death.

"When it comes down to it, I tell them you can't put just any-one in the operating room," Jason reveals. "We have to put people there that are not only competent but know how to work under stress because those are stressful situations. If there's an aneu-rysm that I'm dealing with and the aneurysm ruptures, it's one thing to know the instruments but it's something else to be able to assemble and pass those instruments to the surgeon in a very efficient way, otherwise the patient can expire right in front of you."

Jason says that he frequently tells the room one of his favorite quotes by the ancient Greek poet and soldier Archilochus. It is one that is learned by every member of the Navy Seals: "Under pressure we don't rise to the level of our expectations. We fall to the level of our training. That's why we train hard!"

He uses that statement to reinforce why training is absolutely crucial.

He explains it this way: "If you work hard at something and train hard, it becomes instinctive. Then, in the excitement of the event, you can fall back on your instincts and your instincts are going to carry you through. You don't have to sit and think. I believe that when you start trying to connect the dots in the setting of a stressful situation, you're going to be confused. You're going to be flustered and you're not going to know what to do.

"But if it's like a second nature to you and you know it like the back of your hand, it's instinctual. For example, you're going to know that if you're under water for too long you're going to come up for air. You don't have to look around and think about it. Or you come to a stop sign, you stop. No matter what's going on in the car, you're going to know instinctively, 'I'm coming to an area where I need to stop and I'm going to stop.' You may be still multitasking at the time, but your right foot knows what to do."

It is easy to see a direct line between ball-player Jason and Doctor Jason. Young Jason would train, practice and endlessly repeat every move until it became second nature on the basketball court at high school and LSU. Now Jason instinctively reacts to every incident in O.R. however unexpected it might be.

CHAPTER 33

Just in case...

> *"Are you kidding me? A ventral diastematomyelia dural repair? It appeared absolutely perfect."* – Mark Hadley, MD

JASON TELLS AN INTERESTING story about himself that sheds some light on his attitude to everything he does.

"I was wondering one day why I would keep certain things," he recalls. "I guess I'm sort of a hoarder because I keep screws. If I'm putting something together and there are extra screws, I'll keep them in another box. My fiancée was joking with me. She said, 'You always keep paper napkins, you keep extra screws or bolts or something.' And I said, 'Yeah, it's for just in case.'

"That's my phrase: 'It's just in case.' I might not use that screw for this project, but it could be perfect for the next project. Or I might not have a spill this time but there might be a spill in the car when we're somewhere else, so I keep napkins in my pocket.

"I remember even when I was playing basketball, I would carry so many things in my pocket. Even when we had a kind of a musical group when I was in college, they would nickname me 'Pockets' because I always had stuff in my pockets. It was 'just in case.' If something happened, I would be ready for those 'just in case' moments where your body and your instincts take over."

With surgery, there are a lot of 'just in case' moments.

Dr. Mark Hadley, the neurosurgery specialist and professor under whom Jason trained at UAB, specializes in the treatment of spinal column and spinal cord disorders. He shared a notable story about his former student.

"One day, I received a photograph on my iPhone," he said. "I'm looking at it and recognized it was from Jason. I texted back and said, 'Is that the ventral dural closure of a diastematomyelia?'

"Now that is one of the hardest developmental entities to treat in the human spinal cord. It's a congenital developmental anomaly of the human spinal column and spinal cord where a spinal vertebra has not segmented properly in utero and has formed two spinal canals with a fibrous or bony septum separating them at one or more levels instead of a single spinal canal."

Dr. Hadley explained the complex procedure in some detail, summarized briefly here. "The surgeon must resect anything that's in the middle, between the two hemi cords to release the spinal cord. When this complex and risky microscopic portion of the procedure is completed, the surgeon then has to sew up the dorsal part of the dura, the lining, over the back of the cord. That's the way this type of spinal cord detethering procedure is done. I have done seven diastem detethering procedures in 129 spinal cord tethered patients I've treated in thirty-two years. They are very unusual. One of those patients I treated with a diastem included Dr. Cormier as my resident assistant during his sixth year of his training.

"He'd just sent me the picture without text or explanation. I texted him and said 'Are you kidding me? A ventral diastem dural repair?' His photographic representation of his resection and ventral dural repair appeared absolutely perfect."

A moment later, Dr. Hadley received another text from Jason. "He replied, 'Yes it was. Thanks Dad!'"

Jason had stored away that knowledge – 'just in case' – while assisting Dr. Hadley and was able to draw on that experience when performing the complex and risky procedure in his own practice. Those days of 'helping dad out' in Birmingham had led to a life restored in Lafayette.

Dr. Hadley reached out to Jason to be involved in an organization that provides transition training for residents about to move on to professional practice.

"We try to cover all those bases, so we get speakers but we don't want old guys like me," he said candidly. "We want young people who say, 'Look, I got out four years ago and I was scared to death and I didn't have this, I didn't have that, and this is what I did.' I invited Jason to serve as a faculty member and course director. I thought he was ideal for that and of course he was terrific at it. He's a remarkable contributor."

CHAPTER 34

Pulled over by the cops

"It was very scary, and for a second I really felt like my life was in danger." – Jason Cormier

JUST WHEN THINGS SEEM to be going great, Life has a habit of throwing a monkey wrench into the works.

For Jason, one such event occurred a few years after he started his neurosurgery practice and was well on his way to a successful career. Then something happened that had the potential to derail everything that he had worked so long and so hard to achieve.

"I was getting set to go to Miami where I would participate in and teach a cadaver lab," he recalls. "I was coming off a really good week and things were going in the right direction for me professionally. I had a feeling that all the decisions that I was making were basically for the best and they were working out and things were going well."

The evening before the Miami trip, Jason met up with some friends at a local restaurant for dinner and some drinks. "I was certainly not in any way intoxicated by any means," he stipulates, and he knew he had an early start set for the following day. "I had to catch a plane at 6:30 a.m. that next morning to go to Atlanta then on to Miami which is where the cadaver lab was being held and things were set up there for me to do it and teach it."

He was out with a few buddies that he hadn't seen in a while. "I'd been just working like crazy and getting some things done in my life professionally and they understood that, building my practice and all that. After dinner, I got to my truck and there were two individuals who were there and also friends of ours and so they said, 'Look, we're ready to go home too, so if you're leaving can you just give us a ride, that would be great.'"

They got into the truck and, with Jason at the wheel, set off on the journey home. A few minutes later, Jason saw the blue lights flashing in his rearview mirror. He was being pulled over by the police. One of the officers approached the truck. He spoke to Jason and went through the usual procedures.

"Then he asked me, 'How much have you had to drink?'" says Jason. "I told him that I had had a couple of glasses of wine, but certainly I didn't feel like I was intoxicated or anything like that. I said, 'Was I speeding?' He said, 'No, but you were swerving, or you accelerated or something, so I pulled you over.'"

The officer said that he needed Jason to get out of the vehicle. "So I got out, did the sobriety test and then the other officer, the female officer, said, 'I'm going to have to get you to come down to one of our units.' I said, 'Excuse me?' And she said, 'Yes, you have to come down to do a Breathalyzer test.'"

Jason was beginning to feel a trace of anxiety, but at the same, he was confident that he was sober and the Breathalyzer test wouldn't be a problem.

"I said, 'Okay, whatever you guys need to do, I want to cooperate.' So we went down to this place where they keep these things. I blew into the Breathalyzer and it said 'error,' and I said, 'Well, I guess you got your answer.' He said, 'No, no, you have to do it again.' And at this point in time, I'm thinking, okay this is a little weird. I'm not really sure why I'm being asked to do this multiple times. So I did it again and the officer said, 'Oh, you're over the limit.'"

Jason was shocked to hear those words. "I'm like, 'Wait, what? You're kidding me!'" Jason says that he didn't see actual results on the Breathalyzer unit. "At this point I'm thinking, 'Wow, this is crazy. I know I didn't drink that much.' But, you know, I'm in their custody so I'm just going to go along with it.'"

Jason called his attorney who told him that the police would take him downtown and explained what would happen. He also told Jason that he would make arrangements and get him bonded out.

Jason felt his heart sink. "I remember being inside the squad car and I'd never been in a squad car in my life," he recalls. "I'm thinking to myself, 'Gosh, this is really scary.' Like, I'm really terrified for my life. As much as I hate to say it, you know, you start thinking about these stories you hear about people that have been taken to different areas and have been beaten."

He says that these thoughts were racing through his mind even though he had never, in his life, had any bad run-ins with the police. In fact, he had experienced really cordial interactions with police officers, even when he could have been in the wrong. Despite his anxiety, he was thinking – or at least hoping – that it would get sorted out and just go away. But when they got downtown, reality began to sink in.

"Now I'm at the police department, I'm being photographed, the whole nine," he says. "I'm thinking, wow this is all surreal to me. I'm just like, this is crazy, this is weird. And at the time I'm talking to the officer and I was like, 'Look, I've operated on a couple of you guys,' and I'm thinking that they're going to go, 'Well yeah, we know you and this is what happened and it's not gonna be a big deal and then you can go about your way.'"

But that wasn't going to happen. This was a very different experience.

"It was very scary, and for a second I really felt like my life was in danger," Jason admits. "I really felt like something bad was going to happen and at that particular point in time I started praying to myself. 'God, just get me through this, whatever they're going to do to me, just get me through this.' Because, as a Black man, I'm thinking all these different things that could happen. It's really a cultural thing, I guess, and the things that you've heard in the past are still going on today. This was also after a Black man in Texas was killed being pulled behind a truck. So all these things are on my mind and going through my head, not to mention that this particular force didn't have a very good reputation at all."

Eventually the procedure concluded and Jason was released. As he stepped out of the police department, there was an initial feeling of relief.

"I was like, okay, I got out, I wasn't beaten up," is how he puts it. "I never saw the inside of a cell or anything like that. Actually, the officer that made the arrest, she was extremely nice, extremely professional and she was one that said, 'No, you'll need to do the Breathalyzer test, but I mean you look fine.' But when the other officer said, 'Oh no, you're over the limit…' Still today, I don't believe that that reading was correct, but I remain supportive and thankful for the hard work and dedication of all our police officers as they have very demanding jobs."

Jason's feelings of relief were quickly replaced by less positive thoughts as the reality of his situation became apparent to him. "It was probably one of the most degrading things I've ever experienced," he discloses.

Jason's attorney told him that they would be able to take care of the DUI charge and that he would not be convicted, it would go away. But, understanding that Jason was wracked with self-recrimination about the event, he also had some words of support. "He said to me, 'You weren't involved in an accident, you didn't injure anybody, so the first thing you have to do is forgive the man in the mirror,'" Jason recalls. "For me, that was a very important statement he made when he said, 'You're not perfect. Forgive the man in the mirror.'"

He also pointed out that, for many people in the community, Jason is a role model, even if he didn't feel like it at that particular moment. As such, an incident like this can have an even greater impact emotionally and psychologically than it would on most people. He reminded Jason that, as he became more established, there would be people who took pleasure in seeing him brought low. Maybe there had been some of those people in the restaurant prior to the traffic stop.

As a doctor, Jason is subject to very close scrutiny with regard to anything that might affect his abilities.

"The Medical Board is very strict about those things and they pretty much dropped the hammer on me," he notes. "I was forced to undergo monitoring every single day. You have randomized testing to make sure there's nothing in your system and this went on for two years."

The testing itself wasn't a problem because Jason is not an alcoholic. He understood that it's a regimen put in place because the Medical Board wants to make sure physicians take this seriously. "I accepted that and it cost a lot of money and time away from my clinic," he says. He realizes now that the regimen had a positive effect on his life.

"Through that, not drinking and not going out, it actually took me away from the nightlife and the social life in Lafayette," he says in retrospect. "I had time to focus more on other things. I wasn't spending money or spending time with a lot of people, going to dinners and social events and whatnot. That same year, I was scheduled to take my oral Board exams for neurosurgery and so I started settling down. I was going through the monitoring process which, again, was every day. I was still operating and just abiding by what the Medical Board wanted and that included monitoring and also checking in regularly."

Without the distractions, Jason was fully focused on his surgical practice and preparing for his oral Board exams. Even so, he was still suffering pangs of guilt and sadness about the entire event.

"There were a bunch of people that reached out to me, but I really didn't want to hear from anybody," he admits. "You just want to die when stuff like that happens."

It was words from members of his family that made the entire experience more bearable.

"I was beating myself up like, 'How could you do this?'" he says. "And it came to the point that my own mother finally said, 'Son, you know something? You're not perfect. You have to realize that no one is perfect. This is all in God's control.'

"Once I realized that I said, 'You know, there must be a message in this.' It was my brother John that said, 'God is saying you need to be prepared. There are more things coming your way and you need to be prepared.'"

Without the distractions, Jason was able to focus on the upcoming Medical Board examinations. His focus paid off: "I went through my Board prep and I took the test. I actually achieved the second highest score in the country."

Jason felt that put a lot of things in perspective. "It was like, all right, this is what you need to do."

At the same time, Jason was in active discussions with Mark Gundrum about his involvement with ARCA and NASCAR, as we'll see later. "Those negotiations were moving forward," says Jason. "Shortly after that, I was also talking with Orangetheory about opening up my own Orangetheory location."

There was another benefit of Jason's renewed focus.

"Because I really wasn't dining out or drinking anymore, my physical fitness actually improved," he says. "I was in the best shape of my life. I mean, I felt like I was back playing basketball again at LSU! All of that was really a result of the DUI and its aftermath because it just made me focus so much more and turn away from some of the nonsense I'd gotten involved in.

"It was a lesson that made me a better person in so many ways. So, I felt like there was a message in all of that. I felt like God was saying, 'There are big things coming and I need you to be prepared,' just as my brother had said. With all these things happening almost that same year, I was able to focus, kind of clear my head, hit the reset button and just go after anything, any passion," he says. "I went after it."

Neurosurgery was still at the forefront of what he did. "But, at the same time, I was actually able to see, sort of 'beyond the shadows,' if you will," he says now. "I decided that there's so much more to life. Neurosurgery is not going to be the only thing for me."

Newly energized, Jason would go on to rediscover his love for auto racing and sports safety as well as DJing and making music. At the same time, he was becoming a consultant to several spinal instrumentation companies and being Internationally recognized as a top neurosurgeon and concussion specialist.

"All these things just started going bananas and so that's what did it," says Jason referring to the DUI and the regimen that followed. "It actually allowed me some time to clear my head. Looking back, I was thinking, 'Man, I still feel maybe I shouldn't have gotten it from a legal standpoint.' But from a moral standpoint – and for what it did for me, clearing my head and whatnot – it was one of the best things that ever happened to me."

Reflecting how the incident actually had a positive effect on his life, Jason says, "I responded to it, but I could have just sulked and maybe got another DUI and another one. But I recognized what it was. I listened to my mother when she said, 'Recognize that you're not perfect.' And I remembered my brother's words when he said, 'God is just telling you that you need to be prepared.' At the time, I had no idea what that was all about," he admits.

"I think it all returns to a quote from the British singer-song-writer and rapper Labrinth who said, 'Success takes you where character cannot sustain you.' That, I think, really spells it out. My character wasn't where it needed to be at that particular time, and that kind of woke me up. It made me realize what's truly important and who's on your side, too."

In some ways, Jason had gone through what some people call 'the five stages of grief' as a consequence of the DUI charge. As Jason has said, "You just want to die when stuff like that happens." But he was able to face the challenge, see it as a learning moment and create a positive outcome.

CHAPTER 35

The birth of the Motorsports Safety Group

"He stressed to me that many of the concussions were being overlooked, not just in automobile racing but in general from bicycle falls to people that just get a bump on the head, and because of that, a lot of damage is being done to the brain." – Jeff Goodwin

NEUROSURGERY IS UNDOUBTEDLY Jason Cormier's principal passion as well as his profession. Having said that, he has a second passion: cars, particularly very fast cars. If he isn't in surgery or at his clinic, you are likely to find him at a racetrack or tuning and tweaking his own cars and collection of souped-up go-karts. Watching a race – Formula 1, NASCAR or IndyCar – is fun, but for Jason getting behind the wheel himself is what he really loves.

In recent years, Jason has been able to combine his two passions to benefit drivers by focusing on how to identify and prevent the effects of concussion that result from even seemingly minor accidents.

Even as a kid, Jason had loved cars. His first 'real' car was a gift from his brother John while he was in med school.

"We just did things for each other that helped," said John, who knew Jason could not afford to buy a car. "He didn't have a student loan and he didn't have any money. It was a cool car, that Nissan ZX turbo, and it was modified so it was fast. He said it was that car that helped him when he'd had a rough day, studying

Jason prepares to test-drive a car at the Myrtle Beach, SC, racetrack.

or at work. But the car helped him feel it wasn't that bad and it kind of gave him the strength and motivation to get through some tough times."

Jason's fascination with auto racing inevitably developed into a personal involvement with the sport. As Jason has said, he doesn't actively seek out people but it seems God puts people in his path at exactly the right moment.

Angelique Guidy is not a doctor but as Director of a company called Innovative Surgical Devices, LLC, based in the Birmingham, Alabama area, she has known Jason for many years, initially on a professional basis and later as friends.

"I had a friend, Jeff Goodwin, who was really in with getting sponsorships for ARCA Racing," recalled Angelique.

A little background... Since its inception, ARCA has been a 'stepping-stone' to NASCAR racing. ARCA's premier division is the ARCA Menards Series and many of auto sports' top drivers got their start there. In April 2018, NASCAR fully acquired ARCA.

Angelique had met Jeff Goodwin and Suzzane Skinner – known as "Mama Sue" – almost by chance. "Jeff and I were working together through our racing company, So Good! Entertainment or SGE," said Suzzane. "Jeff has more of the racing background than I do. We were actually at a race having dinner with the race team the night before the race, which was our custom."

Jeff, with his outgoing personality, started talking with Angelique and her husband John. "They struck up the typical friendly conversation that Jeff has with everyone alive and we became friends from that situation to this day with Angelique and John," recalled Suzzane. "She introduced us to several people, one of them being Dr. Cormier."

"Jeff wanted me to help him get sponsorships and work with him," said Angelique. "Once I realized what he did, it hit me that Jason Cormier also loves vehicles and I thought, well, he may enjoy going to one of these races."

"I spent years in motor racing and I was looking to put together a medical platform that we could reach out to the mass audience, at the track as well as off the track," said Jeff. "I asked Angelique, did she have any doctors that had a platform that love automobile racing? And she introduced me to Dr. Cormier."

Angelique picks up the story: "I told Jeff that I would help him and Mama Sue with their sponsorship search, and could he also do me a favor and get Dr. Cormier to a race? I didn't know if that was a difficult request or an easy request as I knew nothing about racing. I just told Jeff what a good friend Jason was to me and how I respected him."

"The first race he attended, I believe, was in Kentucky that September and we actually featured him and his work on one of the race cars that the Venturini Motorsports was racing that week, because Angelique told me all the great things he did," said Jeff. "I think it was his birthday and we had some extra room on the car and I was just fascinated by his heart and his passion for racing, so it was easy to put him on a race car that raced on nationwide TV."

That was something Jason had not expected. "That blew Jason away," said Angelique. "It was a big surprise. I reached out to his sister, Dolores, and she actually got me a picture of his and Dr. Appley's practice, Acadiana Neurosurgery, and so they were able to put that on the car, just as a gesture. Nobody paid for that. It was just that Jeff Goodwin had some people that he was friends with and they just did it as a gesture and it was beautiful."

A few months earlier, Angelique had accompanied Jeff and Suzzane to a race at Daytona, the first race she ever attended, and there were a couple of accidents on the track. She began to ask questions about safety procedures. She was wondering, where are the doctors here and what happens to these injured drivers? "I realized they needed help," she said.

When Jason went to the Kentucky race in September, the timing couldn't have been better.

'It just so happened that there were representatives there for the safety side of racing," noted Angelique. "The safety people that were there, they had not visited that track for, I believe, three years so it really was a fluke. Well, nothing is a coincidence but it's really interesting how that happened. And so that was a God thing. Dr. Cormier, not only is he a racing fan, he's a neurosurgeon that focuses on the spine and the brain so he was already really into concussions and things like that. It was like a puzzle that just fit together beautifully."

Jason saw this as an opportunity to get his message out there. Jeff asked him what that message was.

"He told me that he was born to do what he does and that was to save lives," Jeff recalled. "He stressed to me that many of the concussions were being overlooked, not just in automobile racing but in general from bicycle falls to people that just get a bump on the head, and because of that, a lot of damage is being done to the brain."

Jason explained to Jeff, "I believe if you can help me put together a platform here, I will have a national audience that I can reach, and I just want to do it to help people out."

That was the day that began Jason's hands-on involvement with auto racing. It was the beginning of what would become Motorsports Safety Group.

"When we put that together, we sat in a trailer, actually a hauler, Mark Gundrum, Dr. Cormier, Jeff Goodwin and me," said Angelique. "We sat right there and that's when it started. Mark Gundrum was a huge part of that."

It was the first time that Jason would meet Mark Gundrum, ARCA vice president, Business Development and Corporate Partnership.

"Once we understood who he was as an individual, which was impressive," said Mark, "And his resumé for sure and what his desires and intentions were in the sport of racing, we started to have conversations about would it be a good fit to formalize the relationship between his group and our racing circuit."

During these initial discussions, Mark and his ARCA colleagues wanted to know what Jason and his group's goals and objectives were as they got involved and what they were seeking to accomplish.

"They were very forthright, very positive ideas, very unselfish ideas and goals about seeking to try and help make sure that the sport was educated about safety and was doing what it could to understand injury," Mark noted. "And then help participants understand how they could prepare to prevent injury and how they could diagnose levels of injury on their own, even, to make sure they knew if they had symptoms. And then, of course, once, if injured, how to properly go about recovery.

"We talked about what could Motorsports Safety Group bring to a series like the ARCA Menards Series in addition to concerns of concussion and brain injury and spine injury, those devastating, debilitating injuries, just the everyday opportunities to take care of oneself and be prepared to participate in a sport like auto racing. Hydration, nutrition, exercise, mental fatigue."

"That's how it started," noted Angelique, "And then Jason spoke to his colleague, Dr. Alan Appley, and he was interested, and then Dr. Dani Bidros is one of his best friends in the world and so he asked him to be part of it as well. It was just awesome."

CHAPTER 36

Keeping young drivers safe

"I think Dr. Jason Cormier is everything we want to see in and around NASCAR." – Brandon Thompson

"THE GROUP THAT DR. CORMIER put together were stand-up people, highly regarded in the medical profession," said ARCA's Mark Gundrum. "And Dr. Cormier was kind enough to bring those people to events and then we made arrangements to have those people address our participants."

ARCA is where many young drivers take their first real step toward professional racing. "What Dr. Cormier and his colleagues brought was very valuable to these young racers," said Mark. "Jason and I worked on how this would play out. My role was to get him into the sport and get him in front of the participants, being the drivers and the team owners, and then allow him to build relationships with those participants, to allow those drivers and team owners to gain his trust and vice versa."

Jason developed a series of seminars to help young drivers learn how to stay safe and healthy.

"We would schedule these seminars and we would tell these young drivers, in some cases just fifteen years old, that they had to stay and participate in the seminar after the drivers' meetings," said Mark.

In addition to the seminars, Jason would liaise with track officials and would be on hand during races in the event of an emergency. "If

Jason leads a Motorsports Safety Group seminar for drivers at Daytona International Speedway.

any drivers had wrecks, he could advise them if they had a hit on the head," said Jeff Goodwin. "He was able to use it as a platform that got national attention to be able to speak about his desire to educate people about health safety when it comes to the brain."

Brandon Thompson is NASCAR's Vice President, Diversity and Inclusion. From the start he was a strong supporter of Jason's involvement in the sport and particularly the education he was able to bring to the ARCA drivers. "I think Dr. Jason Cormier is everything we want to see in and around NASCAR," he said. "Obviously, he has a passion for racing, first and most of all. He is very well educated, very sharp, very bright. He is innovative which is literally one of our core brand pillars here at NASCAR. And look, let's not dance around the fact that he's a Black man. And so I think that when you put those things together, knowing the background that he has in sports and some of the connections that he has, he's everything we want and need in NASCAR as we try to build a more diverse and inclusive community."

Having seen Jason leading seminars with the young drivers, Thompson could see that he was able to communicate the importance of avoiding head trauma. "When you're talking to these drivers, their focus is all over the place because a lot of these seminars are happening on race day, so you know drivers, by nature, are always moving," he said. "This whole thing, the notion of speed, for them is at the forefront of their minds at all times. So when you have their attention, you have to do something to hold that attention and he is able to do that, because the information is intriguing, but he presents it in a way that they can understand it and absorb it."

Thompson summed up Jason's approach to the seminars this way: "He's easy to talk to. He's down to earth, you know; he's not talking down at you or preaching at you. He's able to give you good information in a very natural and organic way."

This is where another Brandon – Brandon Rochon – comes into the story. Brandon's brother PJ had been Jason's roommate at medical school in New Orleans, and when Jason was putting together his Motorsports business, he reached out to him for some help with graphic design and marketing. Brandon Rochon traveled with Jason on many occasions and saw him interact with the drivers during the seminars.

"This is the ARCA circuit and these are younger teenagers; maybe fifteen, sixteen, years old," said Rochon. "They will come up to him and say things like, 'Are you really a brain surgeon? You really open up brains every day?' And he was like, 'Yeah.' One of the guys, I remember his name was Zane, and he was like, 'Man, that's really cool but like it's making me nauseous, I want to throw up,' and I could see Doc chuckle at that because a gap was bridged. You had someone who would be too intimidated to speak to a surgeon, but then Doc's talking about, you know, cambering a car and slipstreaming and differentials and ratios and talking like 'gearhead talk' to another racer. They think that's really, really cool, because typically you don't have someone with the stature of being so medically-trained as to be a brain surgeon, a neurosurgeon, and also have the skill-set, the patience and also just the down-to-earth-ness to still be a racer and converse with people like that. I thought that was a pretty cool thing but it was kinda unbelievable. Like people wouldn't believe that he was a brain surgeon behind the wheel of a NASCAR car. It's kinda crazy!"

CHAPTER 37

From the track to tumor surgery

"Everybody that we meet in life, I think there's a reason why
God introduces us." – Angelique Guidy

JASON WAS BECOMING MORE involved with auto racing, both as a fan and an advocate for brain safety for the drivers. Both Jeff Goodwin and Angelique Guidy recalled a remarkable incident that was certainly a case of being in the right place at the right time.

Jeff and his business partner, Suzzane Skinner of So Good! Entertainment, were at a race in Atlanta. They had recently landed a major client as a sponsor and Angelique was helping Jeff and Suzzane on an unpaid basis.

"I got very close to Steve, one of the client's executives, and his wife Kiki," said Jeff. "They had a daughter that had been declining because she had a tumor that was deep in the brain and she was starting to have a lot of spasms, days in bed, sickness. Steve and I, we started kind of having a prayer, just praying for his daughter and I started learning more about this. I believe that they had taken her to four or five doctors and all of them said that the tumor, I believe, was too deep in the brain and it was growing."

Angelique also met with Kiki at the race. "You know there are not that many females that are at these races," Angelique pointed out. "We connected and hit it off and I gave her my phone number. Then she called me the next week."

Kiki said her daughter was only twenty years old and she was going to get an MRI. Angelique shared this with Jason who said that was a good move. However, he said that it was important that it should be a 'with-and-without-contrast' MRI. "I told her that and asked her to get me the results," said Angelique. "She sent me the MRI results to my house in Alabama and I drove them up with me to Nashville."

"We had worked hard to bring ARCA racing back to the Nashville Fairgrounds and we had an upcoming race," said Jeff. "Dr. Cormier was going to be coming to Nashville. We had told him about Steve and Kiki's daughter and he said, 'I need to get involved in this. Let me see all the information.'"

Jeff noted that on the morning of the race, a lot of people wanted Jason's time and attention and this could be a vital part of his developing involvement with auto racing, both for him personally and for Motorsports Safety Group.

"During breakfast I told Jason I had those results with me," said Angelique, "And he asked to look at them."

"Now, this was going to be an important race for him to inter-act with safety officials and so forth," added Jeff, "But he put everything on hold just to take this young lady and make her his priority."

He reviewed the results and asked Angelique to call Kiki. "Right there on the spot I called her," said Angelique. "I handed Dr. Cormier the phone and he spoke to her for approximately forty-five minutes."

Angelique vividly recalls the conversation. "He said, 'There are five people, five practices in the world that I know of that do this type of surgery.' And he asked her, 'Where do you live?' And she lives in Ohio and he said, 'Okay, I would recommend this place as it is the closest one to you.' And then she said, 'Well, great, we could go there.' And then she said, 'What about the other four?' And he named three, and she said, 'Well, that's four, but you told me there were five. Who's the fifth surgeon that can do this type of surgery?' And he said, 'Well, that would be me.'"

Kiki and Steve quickly accepted Jason's offer to do their daughter's surgery. "I helped them coordinate with his office manager in Lafayette," said Angelique. "I said to Dr. Cormier, 'You know they're coming from Ohio. I'm not sure what kind of insurance they have or anything.' And he – verbatim – he said, 'I'm not concerned about their insurance. Just get them here.' He did not recommend her flying so they drove from Ohio. It was Easter week and they drove over and he did this really intricate surgery."

"Jason asked me to pray for him," Jeff recalled. "He said it was a very intense surgery. It was hours and hours in the operating room. I was in Nashville at the time, but I was getting updates on the progress. After it was over with, he talked about how she's going to have some rough days because he had to go so deep in the brain. He pretty much stayed with her day and night for a couple of days. I'd get updates on how she was doing, but he'd already told everybody this is what's to be expected. He called every shot, every single shot, up to the surgery and after the surgery.

"I think that was so important to do because he prepared this young lady's mom and dad mentally for what they were going to have to go through after the surgery. And I thought, 'Man! That's going the extra mile.' The daughter had a very rough go but when they would get a little bit nervous or scared and she was having bad days, he said this was to be expected but this is where we're at. After a few weeks in the hospital, she made a complete turnaround. A couple of months of rehabilitation and she is a walking miracle."

Angelique has had time to reflect on the way that wonderful outcome happened and how all the pieces began to come together at a racetrack. "A lot of times at church, maybe you just go in and you go out, but you know when God speaks directly to you," she said. "And for me, that was the 'Aha' moment. He treated her; she was special. She was not treated like a number. There was a reason why we were all at that race and there's a reason why we all connected."

Jeff shares Angelique's feelings and describes the sequence of events as a "true miracle" that he simply played a small role in. "I had always wanted to put together a medical platform in racing and I think that I didn't realize how big this was until I actually saw a life that was saved by his hands. If Steve's company had not got into racing, I wouldn't have known about it, and if I hadn't been looking for a medical platform, I wouldn't have met Angelique and then found Jason. I believe that the Good Lord had a plan to bring everybody together just to save this one girl's life."

"Everybody that we meet in life, I think there's a reason why God introduces us," was how Angelique described it.

On a lighter note, ARCA Vice President Mark Gundrum recalled a busy day at Chicagoland Speedway. "It's a big NASCAR track and I was responsible for that day's sponsor. I believe it was Kimberly Clark, a pretty big blue-chip company, and I was trying to get the reps rounded up to introduce them to the track president before the drivers' meeting. While I was working to do this, I saw Dr. Cormier and his group come in. They were going to give a seminar after this meeting. I said Hi and I asked him, 'Dr. Cormier, have you ever met Scott Paddock, the track president here in Chicagoland Speedway?' And those two guys looked at each other and they went, 'Yeah, we know each other.' And I was, like, how in the world is that possible? Well, it comes to be that Jason played basketball at LSU and Scott Paddock played basketball at Notre Dame and they had played against each other! So these two guys get reconnected years after their playing careers were over and I could hardly get them apart."

"We had Jason on the cover of NASCAR magazine," said Jeff Goodwin, "But everything we did wasn't to build his ego or to promote him just as a person. He was always, 'Jeff, I want to promote safety and I want people to know that they've got to educate themselves about bumps on the head. You can't take those things lightly.' Every move that was ever made that I've been a part in, he always wanted to know, 'How do we get the message out?' It wasn't about how do we get me out there but how do we get the message out."

CHAPTER 38

The biggest, baddest racetrack in the nation

"They told me, 'This guy has the ability to be a racecar driver.' He was running perfect lines and the car wouldn't go any faster." – Jeff Goodwin

FOR JASON, TALKING TO drivers in seminars would never be enough. Driving is his passion and competitive driving is even better. "He races go-karts professionally," said Jeff in amazement, "And to me, that is suicide! Driving a go-kart at 100 plus miles an hour, maybe 150 at times! If you go to his house, you will see all these go-karts. Not only can he drive them, he knows how to take them apart and how to set them up. He told me, 'I want to know every part of it, everything about it.' So he could probably build one of these with his eyes closed, because he wants to know every piece of it, how it works and how it operates."

As much as he enjoys working on and racing go-karts, it doesn't quite match the thrill of driving a NASCAR-style vehicle. He talked to Jeff about how to make that happen and Jeff told him about the various race car driving schools around the country, but Jason only wanted to drive at Talladega.

"I reminded him that Talladega is the biggest and baddest racetrack in the nation and the banks are like five stories tall," Jeff recalled. "And he said, 'I know. I want to race and I want to go to the very top.

There's no other place that high so that's why I want Talladega.'

Jeff took a deep breath, shrugged and said, "Okay, go for it, big guy."

Jason went to Talladega and a few days later, Jeff got a call from the organizers of the Dale Jarrett Experience. "They told me, 'This guy has the ability to be a racecar driver.' He was running perfect lines and the car wouldn't go any faster. He was going probably 160, 170, and he was getting more out of the car than anybody they had seen. I was just blown away by that. They were calling me and they were so impressed with him."

Later, Jeff asked Jason about the experience, "But when he tells me all about it, he's just so calm. He said, 'Oh yeah, I did that. We did pretty good.' You know he did great, but he doesn't build himself up as far as his ego is concerned. He lets his work do the speaking for him. That's another thing that I admire about him. He carries himself with confidence and he's got to have that confidence because he couldn't be who he is without it."

Brandon Rochon recalled many conversations with Jason when they traveled together or were waiting at a track before a race. "There's eight, nine hours of waiting for a race to pop off," said Rochon. "There's a lot of down time where we were able to chat." They talked about the kind of mindset needed to be a surgeon in the O.R.

"He did explain to me that in the operating room, he has to have a certain type of demeanor if the artery is cut or something," said Rochon. "For the lack of better terms, he has to stay calm, keep that fear factor down to still manage and take care of that patient whose life it is that's on the table. He explained to me about taking a tumor out. You have two minutes to clip an aneurysm and re-suture it or you know your patient will bleed out and flatline. He told me his longest surgery was like twenty-three hours or so with zero breaks, like it was nonstop."

*Jason adds his autograph to the finish line at
Daytona International Speedway.*

Jason maintains an air of calm confidence in the O.R. But Brandon Rochon has also seen another side to his demeanor. "We were going to a race in Charlotte," he said. "Doc had a speaking engagement to do and typically when we land, we rent a car and we just have to sign in where we get our passes, go through the tunnel, follow all the emergency response through a normal race scenario. That day, we were going through all of those tasks to get settled on the track side and he's on the phone with someone back at the hospital and there's an issue with a patient.

"I heard him get upset and his demeanor changed but it was on a different side of a situation. He was ready to make heads roll at the hospital. He was ready to get on the next flight out and go back home to see about his patient. Because after he operates or deals with a patient, they are in the care of someone else when he's not in the room, but he's still ultimately responsible for that particular patient. I don't know what the issue was, but the way that he handled it, he said, 'I will get on the next plane home should I have to, but I expect XYZ to be done and I want confirmation of it immediately!' He was able to split his passion of racing, being at the track and still handle business back at home. But he was ready to kinda navigate 'go left, go right' wherever he needed to be."

It was apparent to Rochon that Jason's priority would always be his patient. "In that regard his demeanor is almost like a lion," he says. "It's like the fearlessness of, 'If I touch it, I want it to be the best it can possibly be. And if it's down to a patient, I want to save that patient's life and make the patient feel and be better.' When I saw something interfere with that, I saw a different side of him that, let's say, wouldn't typically match his 'bedside manner' per se."

Jeff Goodwin is certain about one thing. "He's changed my life forever. He's in my life forever, and I really believe that young lady's life was saved by his talents." Jeff paused thoughtfully for a moment, then added, "Maybe that's the reason I was in racing all those years, because of how he saved her life when, I think, five other doctors gave up on her."

CHAPTER 39

The collar that reduces 'brain slosh'

"Today's action provides an additional piece of protective equipment athletes can wear when playing sports to help protect their brains from the effects of repetitive head impacts." – Christopher M. Loftus, M.D.

DRIVING A CAR AT high speed is not the only way to sustain injuries to the head and neck, but it was his passion for both motor sports and brain safety that drew Jason to a remarkable new device called the Q-Collar.

A concussion can occur when the head receives a direct impact or is subjected to sudden acceleration and deceleration causing the brain to move suddenly and collide with the skull.

However, even seemingly trivial 'bumps' caused by a fall or a collision of heads in a soccer game can have a negative impact on one's quality of life. Doctors call these bumps 'sub-concussive' head impacts that can result in everything from headaches, confusion and fatigue to dizziness, lack of orientation, inability to concentrate and decreased reaction time.

Jason knew that any of those symptoms could lead to a fatal result for anyone driving a vehicle of any sort, on or off the track. But now, beyond the racetrack, coaches – at both the professional and youth sports level – are taking the dangers of concussion and sub-concussive impacts more seriously than in past years. There is also a greater understanding of the long-term effects of neck and spinal injuries from sporting activities.

As a neurosurgeon, Jason uses his skill to work on patients after they have received a brain or spine injury. However, he has become increasingly focused on preventing those injuries before they happen.

Hundreds of hours spent at racetracks, working with the drivers – including the young drivers on the ARCA circuit – as well his involvement with the ongoing research at the Society for Brain Mapping & Therapeutics (SBMT) has increased his focus on preventing and diminishing brain injuries in sports. Rather like breakthroughs in NASA's space program, developments that start in the professional sports arena can trickle down to benefit people in their everyday lives.

One such innovation is the Q-Collar. Doctors refer to the movement of the brain within the skull as "slosh," a key cause of structural changes to the brain. Medical experts have long recognized that eliminating or reducing slosh is essential for long-term brain health for anyone involved in contact sports or similar at-risk activities.

The Q-Collar is a deceptively simple and unobtrusive device that helps stabilize the brain by applying light pressure to the jugular veins. This pressure slightly increases blood volume inside the skull and helps reduce the brain's movement – which is a primary cause of brain injuries. In doing so, the Q-Collar aids in the protection of the brain from effects associated with repetitive sub-concussive head impacts.

Jason was not involved in the creation of the Q-Collar but quickly became an enthusiastic advocate. "They were off the ground before I came on board and I got involved in the third quarter, if you will," he explains. "They had a couple of people in the NFL already wearing the Q-Collar, so the technology was already in place."

By this time, Jason's major project, Motorsport Safety Group, was up and running and he had seen first-hand how racecar drivers, including the teenage ARCA novice drivers, often take repeated jarring bumps. With the help of Dr Julian Bailes, he was connected to the developers of the Q-Collar and expressed his interest in getting involved.

For any innovation related to healthcare, approval by the Federal Drug Administration (FDA) is essential for widespread acceptance by sports authorities, schools and the general public. According to the FDA, from 2006 to 2014, the number of emergency department visits, hospitalizations, and deaths related to traumatic brain injury (TBI) increased by 53%. It is estimated that anywhere from 1.6 million to 3.8 million sports- and recreation-related TBIs occur in the United States annually.

Achieving FDA approval is a convoluted procedure and the Q-Collar creators were finding the process particularly challenging.

When Jason approached the developers of the Q-Collar, they could see that Motorsport Safety Group was a respected organization with goals similar to their own. In addition to Jason himself, MSG's Medical Advisory board includes Dr. Julian Bailes, Dr. Mark Hadley and other nationally recognized experts in the field of neurological wellbeing.

"I was convinced with the technology behind the Q-Collar and reviewed it with Dr Julian [Bailes]," says Jason. "We talked to the Q-Collar team and it was decided that my involvement could be a synergistic relationship wherein I could push this through the racing organizations that I was already involved in. That included NASCAR, the National Hot Rod Association (NHRA) and the International Council of Motorsport Sciences [ICMS]. We were going to attempt to increase awareness that way."

Jason remembers when the developers were trying to get the Q-Collar approved by the FDA: "I was about to do a presentation

Jason explains the benefits of the Q-Collar to champion jockey Johnny
Velasquez at Churchill Downs, KY, during the
'A Night at the Downs' event.

at the Jockeys' Guild in 2017. It was part of MSG's platform about safety in sport and injury protection. I was on the same panel with Jeff Crandall, Chair of the NFL's engineering committee and Director of the UVA Center for applied Biomechanics, and I took the opportunity to introduce the Q-Collar because I really believed in it. I had spoken to Julian just prior to that and that's where the whole concept of bringing the Collar on board into the Motorsport Safety Group initiative became a reality. I was looking for technology that would help prevent head injury, because there was really nothing out there that was all that convincing."

Jason has strong opinions about the effectiveness of most sport safety equipment. "We knew that the helmets were just a false sense of security, outside of providing some protection against skull fractures and skin laceration, the helmets are not effectively protecting the brain," he says frankly. "The Q-Collar is based on the physiology of the woodpecker and the battle ram. We have some things in common with those two animals that particularly strike their heads. It only makes sense to base brain protection on animals that strike their heads that have that inherently as part of their anatomy. It's something that they do every day."

With Jason and MSG on board, the people at Q-Collar would continue to focus on certain areas, such as football, where they already had inroads. "From my standpoint, I was personally interested in auto racing but also all levels and atmospheres of high contact sports, so it made sense that I became involved," he explains. "So with that, in some ways, we approached the FDA together and they started having some more progress."

The FDA had more questions, but they were able to work through them with Jason on board. "From that standpoint," he says, "I became part of the Medical Advisory Committee and helped push the Q-Collar, at least in the racing organizations, and now many other organizations are interested."

In addition to the science, the presence of experts such as Dr. Cormier and Dr. Bailes added to the validity of the Q-Collar.

On February 26, 2021, the U.S. Food and Drug Administration authorized the marketing of the Q-Collar. In a press release issued on that date, the FDA described the Q-Collar as: "a new device intended to be worn around the neck of athletes aged 13 years and older during sports activities to aid in the protection of the brain from the effects associated with repetitive sub-concussive head impacts."

The FDA announcement also included the following quote:

"Today's action provides an additional piece of protective equipment athletes can wear when playing sports to help protect their brains from the effects of repetitive head impacts while still wearing the personal protective equipment associated with the sport," said Christopher M. Loftus, M.D., acting director of the Office of Neurological and Physical Medicine Devices in the FDA's Center for Devices and Radiological Health.

"Even before it was FDA approved, local high schools here in my town were using it," states Jason. We had to sign waivers and be under an IRB. That's an Institutional Review Board that reviews research involving human subjects. There was a kid that had decided to wear it. He had headaches every day after practice, even running simple drills, like running the fifty-yard dash. He was coming home with headaches and after wearing the Q-Collar, he went his entire season and didn't have any headaches at all. And now he's on the map for a college scholarship this year. That's just one of several stories. It's been used in more than 2,800 football games and the results are really remarkable. They're demonstrating the reduction of injuries to the brain by over eighty percent."

On a personal note, Jason adds, "I always wear a Q-Collar when I'm driving."

CHAPTER 40

Leading the brain mapping team

"We are looking at technologies that are just mind-bog-gling, not only for the brain but also the spinal cord." – Jason Cormier

KNOWING THE IMPORTANCE OF increasing his knowledge to keep up with new developments in surgery and medical research, Jason maintains active memberships in numerous societies and organizations.

After several years as a member, he was elected to the position of President of the Society for Brain Mapping & Therapeutics (SBMT) for 2021 – 2022. The SBMT has fostered dramatic advances in brain measurement and therapy by bringing together a wide-ranging group of doctors, scientists, educators, innovators and world leaders. One of their major goals is advancing the science and technology of brain science, an area in which Jason has been actively involved.

It is a reflection of Jason's capability and reputation that he should be selected to lead such a prestigious international society. Describing his involvement with SBMT, he notes, "You are networking with people from Italy, Japan, Korea, China, Russia, really all over the globe, and you're collaborating with scientists, literally, from around the world."

As president, Jason participates in weekly Zoom meetings keeping up to date on what is happening both in the USA and overseas. "The SBMT is active in Washington pushing policies that are going to help not only diagnose different diseases that have become more and more challenging as we move forward but also treatment of these types of diseases," he says with obvious enthusiasm. "Some of these brain initiatives have research budgets that are as much as $4.5 billion."

Describing some of the SBMT's activities, he says, "We're involved in artificial intelligence, virtual reality, trying to design a smart microscope and, of course, brain mapping is at the cornerstone."

Even for someone with Jason's knowledge of brain function, the potential for the advancement of brain health seems almost unlimited. "We are looking at technologies that are just mind-boggling, not only for the brain but also the spinal cord. Really, the whole central nervous system as well as items from the peripheral nervous systems. Brain trauma is going to be one of my biggest platforms as well as the opioid crisis that we're experiencing. We bring in different technologies as well that we feel are going to be promising and proven to help get us through each one of these issues that have been problems for the world for so many years."

From personal doctor visits or watching medical shows on TV, we are familiar with MRIs. However, Jason says SBMT has been involved in the development of diffuse tensor imaging which has become a cornerstone of MRI in terms of the brain's anatomical network of interconnections to dysfunctional areas. Jason explains that this allows doctors to look into the depths of neuronal tissue involved in brain injury that you can't see with a normal MRI.

Perhaps surprisingly, SBMT is working on developments that might not immediately seem connected with brain mapping.

"In September 2020, the Society, along with a number of different scientists and doctors, published the most comprehensive review yet of COVID-19," Jason disclosed. "There are so many different things going on in this international society, and it's just truly a blessing and an honor to be not only associated with it but now to be president."

CHAPTER 41

Music passion reawakened

"I just play music that I think will make people feel good."
– Hadley Castille

MEDICAL TRAINING IS EXTREMELY INTENSE. As with anything Jason undertakes, he focused all his energy and attention on mastering his chosen field of neurosurgery. After leaving UAB, his entire focus evolved into starting and building his practice. His other passion – music – hadn't died. It was simply hibernating waiting for him to awaken it again.

One day, the family of Hadley Castille called Jason's office in Lafayette and asked for an appointment. Hadley Castille enjoyed a decades-long career as a renowned Cajun fiddler with a major fan-following in the United States, Canada and Europe. He was inducted into the Louisiana Hall of Fame and received the Acadiana Folk Heritage Award, among many other accolades.

"He had a very bad, very aggressive tumor that was inoperable," Jason recalls. "We did a biopsy on it and it was a malignancy."

Although surgery was not a viable option, Jason and Hadley formed a bond of friendship that lasted for the rest of Hadley's life.

"I saw him many times after that before he unfortunately passed away," says Jason. "We had really in-depth conversations about life. Actually, his granddaughter, Sarah Jayde Williams, is now really big on the Cajun fiddler scene."

Inevitably, their wide-ranging conversations would include their mutual love for music and Hadley shared many of his musical memories.

"He would tell me so many things," says Jason. "He said, 'Once upon a time I got to play a Stradivarius,' which are the most valuable and highly-prized violins in the world. He said, 'I could never own one, but I've played one.' Hadley got into the story of how a physician apparently owned this Stradivarius and they brought it to him. There were five or six people who were escorting the violin because of its value. He told me that he played it and it was just a beautiful instrument. He was so humble. He said, 'I didn't feel that I was worthy enough to play this thing because it was so great.' And I said, 'Man! You're in the Hall of Fame! What do you mean?' He said, 'I don't really believe that I'm a great fiddler. I just play music that I think will make people feel good.'"

That was a comment that resonated with Jason.

"That's what our conversations were about," he says. "Just like, 'Be true to yourself and follow your heart.' It was never really about, 'How long do I have to live? How bad is this or that?'"

Jason remembers one particular conversation. "Hadley said, 'I had a dream last night. God said I'm gonna be okay.' And this is as the tumor was progressing. It was always just this peace that he had. I learned a lot in the short time that we spent together."

When news of Hadley Castille's illness spread amongst his fans, many people from around the world would call to check on him. "They would ask questions about him, but of course, as his doctor, I couldn't really say anything," says Jason.

During their talks, Hadley shared his knowledge and musical memories with Jason, including stories about Lafayette's music heritage. "I found out that there was so much more music here and its history, too," says Jason. "There are layers and layers and layers of music here. Louis Armstrong, for example. One of the attorneys that I know well bought a place where Armstrong had resided and played a lot of music here in Lafayette. And to find out there were several Grammy award winners from Lafayette, it was just, 'Wow, I didn't expect that.'"

Hadley, with the natural curiosity of a songwriter and storyteller, was interested to hear about Jason's life, too. "I would share with him stories of my experiences in med school and coming up and also my experiences in music and how, at that particular time, I wanted to get back to music because I hadn't gotten back to it yet."

Conversations with Hadley reawakened Jason's love of creating music of his own. "I started thinking to myself, 'Man, why did I ever abandon that?' Of course, I couldn't really afford to get the equipment that I really wanted in my teens. And after that, I was focused on just becoming a good neurosurgeon and honing my skills and sharpening my whole skill set."

He had pushed music to the back of his mind until he started to attend the Hangout Music Fest in Alabama. The three-day annual festival is held on the public beaches of Gulf Shores, Alabama, and features music from multiple genres including rock, indie, hip-hop and electronic dance music (EDM).

"That's what did it for me," recalls Jason. "It was like everyone in the crowd just felt great. It was the EDM DJ Skrillex and I was, like, 'Man! All these people have forgotten about all their problems and they just feel great!' They're bobbing and they're dancing and all that matters is that I'm in a place of fun and happiness and peace."

While he was at the Hangout Fest, he made a pledge to himself. "I said, 'I need to get back to this because with music you can impact even more than one person at one time, and at the same time, it's young music, it's energizing to you as well.' That's what I wanted. I wanted to get back to it and so that's how it came to fruition."

He went online to research what equipment Skrillex and other top DJs were using. "That's it. I acquired all the gear I needed, the tools I needed. And I had to learn the technology to do what I wanted to do. I mean, all the beats and mashups, all that stuff, that I already had in my head. What I needed to learn was the technology to be able to perform."

Jason's new equipment was like a different world compared to the basic turntable and Radio Shack mic that he had used in his teens. With the new technology and his freshly acquired skills, Jason was able to get creative again.

The creativity and the music just flowed from him. He needed a new stage name: his teenage hip-hop name of Cut Master Jay wouldn't cut it anymore. For his music, Jason became CORM!! (in capital letters with two exclamation points).

"Actually, I had no idea what I was going to call myself," he says. "The name came from Doctor Patrick Juneau, a well-known local neurosurgeon. He would just call me 'Corm' and so that's where CORM!! came from."

Since then, he has independently released several EDM albums and created dozens of remixes of songs from artists as diverse as Prince and Jason Aldean, Blake Shelton, Billy Ray Cyrus, Elvie Shane, and many more. He also creates beats and chord progressions for other recording artists. With his 'alter ego' CORM!! He posts updates on Facebook @cormmuzik.

Jason has also combined his love of music with his entrepreneurial spirit. He recently became an investor in 8 Track Endeavors, a Nashville-based entertainment company involved in music publishing, film and TV production, artist management and more. The company celebrated its first Country Radio Airplay chart topper and surprised Jason with his own 'Billboard Number One' plaque for his role/involvement during a celebratory event.

Jason likes to have music playing while he is in surgery, including his own EDM tracks – for certain types of surgery.

Jason received a #1 plaque for his involvement with 8 Track Entertainment when the company achieved its first Airplay chart topper.

"There are different areas of neurosurgery," he explains. "I do a number of procedures, not only the brain but also in the spine. I look at spine surgery like carpentry. It's like you're building or renovating a house. So when I'm 'renovating the house,' so to speak, I want upbeat music, high-energy music and it's just like you're outdoors, building something. Whereas when I'm in the brain, well yeah, I want more Chopin, Bach, Mozart, things like that, so it's a different mindset, essentially. If I'm working on my car, I want hip-hop or EDM or things like that. It's kind of the same way in spine surgery. We're talking as we work in the O.R. but there's high-energy music going on. It's really the mechanics of what you're doing and you're in a different zone."

For Jason, there's a practical benefit of playing music in the O.R. "It also helps you keep track of time too," he says. "You're in one song and you're thinking, 'This is taking me too long' and the song is three minutes and 37 seconds. It also keeps you focused."

He points out the reason for using different types of music for those different areas of surgery: "I couldn't imagine doing spine surgery to Vivaldi. I'd fall asleep!"

CHAPTER 42

Creating music and remixes

"Music is life. That's why our hearts have beats." – Anonymous

WITH HIS REAWAKENED PASSION for creating music, Jason focused on teaching himself the digital techniques that would turn his concepts into reality. He understood that once he had mastered the technical aspects, he would be able to concentrate on the creativity.

For many people, Electronic Dance Music (EDM) might be an unknown entity. Others might be fans of the music but don't know how they could create their own EDM tracks. In his alter ego as CORM!! Jason enjoys sharing details about his musical experience.

His excitement is apparent when he talks about his approach to creating music. "First, everything begins with some sort of inspiration," he stipulates. "Every title for a song, typically, is inspired. On occasion, you might see certain things on the Internet that start an idea. You might come across something that another producer had already kind of started or, at least, you look within their song and maybe find some inspiration that sparks an idea you could build on."

He explains how that works. "It might be just a chord, a hook or a build-up and you can see how you could revise that or utilize that in a different way. You have to figure out first why you like it and so what I typically do is I'll listen to it over a period of maybe four or five days. It's got to kind of catch me first, though. There are several things working in concert. There's the chorus, there's a chord progression, the bass line; it all comes together, and then there's the hook."

He believes it's a mistake to focus primarily on the beats. "When you start putting it all together, beats are just beats; it's what you make of it that counts. The beats, really, are just a bunch of things hitting the pad unless it has a nice bass line and it has a good chord progression going with it; you add the right sound effects to it, and echoes in the right spot."

Jason's music, essentially, falls into one of two categories: songs that are entirely his own composition, or remixes of existing songs.

"If it's a song that I'm making for myself – under my own name and not a remix – it's usually the melody that will capture me and this could happen anywhere and anytime," he explains. "Inspiration happens in strange places. It might happen getting out of the shower, it might happen while you're at the dinner table with a bunch of people and you quickly write it down or you hum it into a cell phone. That's a lot of what I used to do, interestingly enough, when I was a DJ for the rap group we had in high school. Whenever we had words that would pop up in our minds, we wrote them down. We'd have words on scraps of paper, we'd have notes on napkins, on paper towels and whatnot. And then we would come back and we'd try to put that to the beats."

Technology has changed the way that Jason and other songwriters keep track of their sudden inspirations.

"In my current situation, it's kind of the same thing in a way but with cell phones," he says. "Nowadays, with a smartphone, I'll just record memos or just hum a memo, essentially, and just speak into the voice recorder and take notes that I want to remember when I get back to my studio where I can lay some things down."

That's when a track begins to take shape. "Once you get your voice memos, your hummed chord progressions or whatever, you finally sit down in front of your computer – I use Ableton Suite as my DAW [Digital Audio Workstation] – and you want to make sure you have the right tools to do some of these things," Jason advises. "Obviously, you really need a keyboard. I have a few of those and you need what they call MIDI systems. A MIDI system is something that talks to the DAW in the same way that the piano or keyboard does. There's even a lot of fancy, catchy toys out there that you can plug in. All these things connect because the whole essence of the MIDI itself is to incorporate or sequence music, play virtual instruments or actual instruments that you have and by sending MIDI data to a computer synthesizer."

He sums it up like this: "I guess a simple way of saying it is that it will interpret that signal and it will come up with the sound. MIDI stands for Musical Instrument Digital Interface."

Jason points out that you're trying to get all these things to communicate into your DAW and then bring them all together and you can then manipulate it however you want to. "They have made it really quite user friendly to do that and they have a lot of chord progressions and plug-ins so that you don't really have to work as hard as some people used to," he says. "Once I get those things together, then I set down the beats. The beats usually are easy but it's the melody that I start off with first. Once I get the melody, that's going to define the movement, the feeling, of the song. After that, it's the beats per minute, or BPM."

Jason describes how different types of music will determine the BPM. "If you're making, say, a dubstep track, then you know you're going to be in, like, the 150 beats per minute range, or if you're making a future house track, you're going to be in the 128 beats per minute range. The BPM are different depending on the type of track you are producing. I think it should all be based on the melody and how you want it to sound; how fast or slow and how you want the music to pivot. Once you get the melodies and chord progressions and then the bass line, the beats follow. It makes it so much easier. What I use for beats, I have what's called Ableton Push II and that's really a fancy MIDI system that can function as a piano, it can function as a big drum machine, you can integrate a TR-808 or whatever you want. Everything's at your fingertips."

With modern technology, producers are no longer limited by the number of tracks they can combine into a song as they were in the days of recording onto magnetic tape.

"You build up all the elements in separate tracks," he explains. "You have a separate track if you're incorporating guitar and another if you're incorporating some sort of piano sound or chords and so on. You separate all those things out in different layers and you're essentially layering the song. One song might have as many as thirty tracks in it. It's like you're actually bringing a bunch of different 'takes' together to build one song or one file. Once you get those all together, then you get into the mix-down and then the mastering process."

That is Jason's brief overview of his creative process, but he is adamant about one point: "I think it all starts from an inspiration and it's not the easiest thing. A lot of times you might hum something into your phone, you listen to it a few times and it doesn't sound so great anymore and you've got to toss that idea. You can't force it. I think every artist will enter this thing that's called writer's block and it's very real. It can be depressing at times because anything you touch you just feel like this doesn't sound right. That is why it's good to have other creativity going on, and for me that's working on remixes of existing songs."

Jason found a way to set aside an original song that just wouldn't come together by redirecting his mind to another creative outlet.

"When I got back into creating music, there were times when I had writer's block while creating my original music and I'd start listening to a song that was out there and I'd be thinking, 'Well, I kinda like it.' But then I'd go on the Internet, I'd go on YouTube and listen to any remixes that had been posted. I'd decide, 'I really don't like that one, I think I can do it better.' So I would take the song and I would strip it down. There are several different programs right now where you can actually strip out the vocals so you have an acapella track which is just the vocal track on its own. There are also websites where you can go in and you can buy the acapellas and they are royalty-free, and you can change the beat and so on. But now, it's easy enough. I just strip the vocals and then create my own bass line, maintain the melodies and the chord progressions but synthesize them a little bit differently."

Jason says that, depending on the song, he might add in some effects then 're-warp' them back into the beats and the song he is re-mixing. It's essential to find the 'hook' of the song, in Jason's opinion, and he finds that in the acapella vocals after he has stripped them from the original mix.

"Once you line up all your 'pegs', so to speak, through the complex-pro sequencing within the warping tools in the DAW, you put that back into the music," he says. "It gives you what the original beats per minute of the song actually were when it was recorded."

He has some words of warning for anyone attempting a remix for the first time. "Let's say, for example, if the song was originally done at 84 beats per minute but you're looking to do it at 120 beats per minute then you run the risk of speeding the song up and changing the pitch and changing the tone.

"However, using the software that's now available, you can actually speed up the tempo and not risk doing those things. You can maintain the same sound of the vocalist in the faster tempo of your mix. You won't change the pitch at all, you won't change the tone and actually you've accelerated it and now you have an EDM banger!" he exclaims.

For Jason and others who want to create their own digital remixes of existing songs, the availability of the current software offers a massive advantage over the traditional method of recording to tape. The many different elements – such as the vocals, musical instruments and effects – are all saved to individual tracks. A single element can be easily changed or deleted while maintaining all the other elements. You can go back and play around with the tracks or make different remix versions of the recording.

Jason was taken by surprise by the positive response he received when he began to make EDM remixes of songs in the Country music genre.

"When I got into Country EDM, I had no idea that it would take off the way it has and Country EDM is really in its infancy," he notes. "No one is really doing it and it started out as kind of just a project. I had a meeting set up to collaborate with a few groups thanks to Noah Gordon and Average Joes Entertainment in Nashville. But before that I said I'm going to mess around with this a little bit and see what I can do with it. It didn't strike me as something that was even going to be anything, but I said, 'let's just see what happens.'"

Jason listened to two Country songs recorded by BoomTown Saints, "Best Part of Tonight" and "Even on a Bad Day."

"I remixed those two songs and when I warped their vocals back into the bass line and the other effects that I added on to it, it was just a really exciting song," he recalls. "When I met with them, they were blown away and they were saying, 'Man, we were about to toss this song. We weren't going to use it anymore.'"

"They were literally asking me if they could use the song, and I said, 'Yeah, it's yours, I just remixed it.' They were like, 'Oh my gosh, we were gonna stop playing it on our tour.' That eventually led up to going to visit them in Nashville for a show and they were very kind enough to announce me to the audience. The song was already good, I feel like I just added a different energy to it and I was humbled by their response."

Jason's perseverance has proved an asset with his song remixing, just as it has in every other aspect of his life. When something doesn't seem to be working, there's a temptation to simply give up. Some remixes seem to come together quickly, says Jason, but others need a lot of reworking before he is satisfied with the result. Often, he will put the project aside – as he does with his original compositions – and switch to another endeavor so he can return to it with a fresh approach. That was the case with the Prince song, "When Doves Cry," one of the first songs Jason remixed.

"I remember trying to remix that song," he says. "It took me about six times to get the remix I have today. With the first five, I was pushing hard because I really, really, really wanted to do the remix of that song. But each one I did, I couldn't listen to it for longer than twenty-four hours because it just didn't sound right. It was just horrible."

He wasn't going to abandon it but he set it aside, knowing he would come back to it. Inspiration was to come from an unlikely source.

"I remember I was at the house of my fiancé, Kaitlyn, and I was getting out of the shower. I think her son was playing a video game and I heard some chords in the melody that resonated with me for some reason. It was something I heard from his Wii game system and the melody just hit me. I quickly grabbed my phone, I hummed it into the phone and then that very night I said, 'I need to go home; this is in my head and I need to lay this track down.' I went home and I was there probably until three or four o'clock in the morning."

He says that originally, doing a remix of "When Doves Cry" was Kaitlyn's idea, telling him she thought it would be a cool song for a remix.

"I pushed and pushed and pushed but attempts one through five failed miserably," Jason admits. "In my opinion, the final one was it. It was the one and that's kind of what set everything off in terms of remixes."

DJ CORM!! spinning

Jason has words of encouragement for others who, like him, have a passion for creating music or remixing other people's songs but don't know how to go about it.

"When you first start, it can be disheartening because there are so many options, so many things, and you're trying to learn the system," he points out. "I give a lot of credit to 343 Labs out of New York. That's where I obtained my training for music production and that's how I started actually producing EDM due to those courses. But it's going to be a struggle. The first track that I ever completed took me probably three or four months. You just have to sit there and deal with it and then once you learn the system it's almost like driving a car. At first, you can drive to your mailbox, and next time you can drive to the store, and so on. If you can get past those hurdles, then it'll take you wherever you want to go. At the same time, inspiration is key. You want to have a reason as to why you're doing it."

Thinking of all the time he invested in the remix of "When Doves Cry," he says, "It wasn't my original song so maybe that was why it took six different tries. I'm not sure. But I know I wanted to make sure that it was something that I could be proud of and I could present to other people and say, 'Look, this is something I did. What do you think?' After listening to that final remix, I was so excited about it that I let Kaitlyn listen to it and she loved it, which to me was and continues to be the final word. She has now become my litmus test, so to speak. After I produce something, I let her listen to it and if she says, 'No, no, no,' then I will typically toss it, go back and remix it."

Jason has had meetings with record companies but has decided he doesn't want to be under any one record company from the start. He remains an independent artist and producer and retains all his own publishing.

"I have a great deal of thanks and appreciation to Preshias Tomes Harris in Nashville for that guidance, as I'm sure many other artists out there now would say as well."

Jason's motivation to make music is not to become famous or to make a fortune.

"I make my music that I think will make people feel good," he says. "I think the music I make is young energy and it keeps you young and vibrant and active. It makes you want to go to the gym when you don't feel like it. It makes you want to get on a boat If you just want to be on the water. It drives you to do certain things at certain points throughout the day, throughout the month, throughout the year, throughout your life."

When Jason talks to someone who is interested in making their own music or doing remixes, he tells them it's a lot easier now than it was a few years ago but he cautions about not investing too much money in equipment right from the start.

"These days, there are so many different things that have made it feasible to make recordings right at your house," he says. "You can build your own studio and you don't have to have, like, 75 different 'toys.' You can really do a lot with just three or four and you have to have speakers, of course. Be prepared to start collecting different types of equipment as you need them. I think I have four DJ controllers now and eight CDJs that are digital turntables. As they upgrade them you can start getting more! I would just caution people to be careful as it can become expensive, but it doesn't have to be. You can do just what you want to do with a lot less. Some people are still using vinyl and they do just fine, so I think of them as the true DJs.

Jason often thinks back to when he was first DJing in high school. "I realized I don't really want to be a rapper and grab the microphone and all that," he says. "But I remember this saying that goes, 'Music is life. That's why our hearts have beats.'"

Jason's interest in music isn't confined to EDM and hip-hop. He finds inspiration and pleasure in multiple musical genres, including songs that have played an important role in his life.

CHAPTER 43

Meeting Evanescence

*"I just happened to mention in one of our conversations
that I was about to cast that video and he flipped out like a
fanboy."* – Suzzane Skinner

JASON IS STILL A FAN of Evanescence, the group whose song,
"Bring Me to Life," had been the inspiration for him to follow
what he realized was his real calling, to become a neurosurgeon.
He has followed their career ever since.

Jason had met Suzzane 'Mama Sue' Skinner when they
worked on the start-up of his Motorsport Safety Group. Suzzane
is involved in many aspects of the entertainment business from
her office in Nashville. One of those aspects is casting for music
videos, and one day she received a call to cast some people to
appear as extras in a video set to shoot in Tennessee.

"I just cast him and his friend in a music video that I didn't
realize was a huge goal for him," said Suzzane. "It was a video for
the song "Use My Voice" by Evanescence, a group that was highly
influential in his life. I just happened to mention in one of our
conversations that I was about to cast that video and he flipped
out like a fanboy and said, 'Oh my gosh! I would love to come
and be in that!' I was pleasantly surprised!"

Even the best-organized video shoots are somewhat chaotic
with lights, cameras and audio equipment attached to cables
snaking among the crew and talent as the producer tries to keep

every shot on schedule.

During a break in the shooting, Jason made his way over to Amy Lee, the lead singer for Evanescence.

"I introduced myself and said I had been invited to be in the video by Mama Sue," recalls Jason. "I told Amy that Evanescence had been instrumental when I decided on my career path in medicine. I believe she had heard that I was a neurosurgeon and she thanked me for telling her that."

He could tell that she was really distracted by the pressure of the video shoot. However, Amy did tell him that the next time he was in Nashville there might be an opportunity to connect and have lunch. At that point, a member of the production team approached Jason.

"She asked me, 'Are you one of the extras? Because normally we don't usually let people just come up,'" notes Jason, "And she's like, 'What do you do?' So I told her and she said, 'You're what? You're a neurosurgeon?' I said, 'Yes, I'm leaving late tonight. We have a flight out at five a.m. I'm in clinic tomorrow morning and surgery tomorrow afternoon.'"

He smiles as he recalls what he describes as a 180 degree change in attitude. "I told her my story and how the Evanescence song had affected me. "She said, 'Okay, just no photographs, no autographs,' and I'm like, 'Okay, I've been on sets before!'"

Jason believes they probably Googled him to see if he really was who he said he was!

Suzzane said it was typical of Jason to bring a friend with him who shared his appreciation of Evanescence. "I've heard so many stories about the generosity that he has, in taking care of patients or just suddenly dropping everything to take care of someone randomly," but she admitted she was surprised that he was so open about the backstory on why he cared about them so much. "He was very excited to be a part of the video," she said, adding, "He got a nice, clear shot in the video, too!"

A screenshot of Jason appearing in the Evanescence music video
for the song "Use My Voice."

Jason has developed a strong attitude of persistence to achieve his goals, one of which was to tell Amy Lee what an impact her song had made in his life. When the opportunity arose, he quickly rearranged his schedule and flew from Lafayette to Nashville to appear in the music video. Once there, he was able to bypass the 'gatekeepers' and talk to Amy. It is probably a conversation that she will remember too. After all, how many people can say they wrote a song that inspired someone to become a neurosurgeon?

CHAPTER 44

Passing the torch of inspiration

"They told me that it was Jason who inspired their son to go and study neurosurgery. It was a touching moment." –
James Ambroise

"JASON IS ONE OF THE most persistent human beings that I've ever met," said his friend Dallas Webb. "When Jason sets his sights on a goal, he's like a laser-focused missile. He goes right at it until he hits his target."

That sense of persistence has influenced Dallas in his own business career.

When Dallas graduated with his MBA, he said the job market was absolutely horrible. "The tech bubble had just exploded so nobody was hiring," he recalled. "I just remembered what Jason did from med school and I was like, 'Alright, you know what. I'm not going to give up!' I was sending out my resume probably fifteen times every single day; even to the same people."

Eventually, through the network he had built up because of his persistence, Dallas managed to find work as an unpaid intern at an investment bank in Boston. "I was in the office every morning at 6:00 a.m. I didn't leave until midnight, probably every day. I was busting my butt and doing it for free. After three months, the Director of Research came to me and he said, 'I've never seen anything like this. We'd like to offer you a job. We can't pay you a lot.' But next thing I know, I had a job."

Dallas drew inspiration from Jason's work ethic and applied it to his own life.

"If I hadn't taken the risk and busted my butt like that, I don't think I'd be where I am today," Dallas admits. "Jason definitely had an impact on my life."

Dallas recalled that he has seen the effect that Jason has on those around him, even complete strangers.

"Jason and my wife and I all went to the Kentucky Derby a couple of years ago," he said. "Jason invited us as he got some good tickets. Even up in the room where all the bigwigs were, people were just coming over to him, people who didn't even know him. Of course, he had a real fancy hat on. You know, with the Kentucky Derby, it's all about the hats and all that, so he had a pretty funky hat on and it garnered a lot of attention. He can walk into a room and light the room up. He's got a magnetic personality. People want to be around him and talk to him. He just has that magic to him. It's really hard to put into words."

After a moment's thought, Dallas summed it up this way: "He's like the sun in the solar system. He walks in the room and people gravitate toward him. It's incredible to watch, to be honest."

James Ambroise recalled an incident that happened in an airport lounge a few years ago. "It was in Dallas, Texas, and this family was sitting at a table next to me," he said. "For some reason we just struck up a conversation, and the guy mentioned that his son, Trey, who was with him, was studying neurosurgery at UAB. I said that a really close friend of mine was a neurosurgeon and had studied at UAB in Alabama and at Duke. The family was from Louisiana and they said, 'Oh really? What's his name?' And I said 'Jason Cormier.' They said, 'Oh, we know Dr. Cormier extremely well.' The father was a doctor and the entire family knew Jason."

The family shared something with James that affected him deeply. "They told me that it was Jason who inspired their son to go and study neurosurgery. It was a touching moment. It made me proud to know Jason and to see what he's accomplished in his life."

The father who was talking with James was none other than Dr. Sam McCluggage who had inspired Jason to avoid every distraction and focus on achieving his goal, with the words, "Only you, yourself, can keep you out of medical school." And now it was Jason who had inspired Dr. McCluggage's son to follow his calling to neurosurgery.

Jason taking a break on the hood of his Hummer H1.

CHAPTER 45

There's more to the Mother's Day story

AT THE BEGINNING of this book you read how Jason made a controversial decision to operate on a critically injured patient that many colleagues believed to be a hopeless case. But it was Mother's Day…

As time passed, Jason was involved in many other surgeries but he maintained an interest in his Mother's Day patient and her son and sister from that terrible car accident. Her husband, meanwhile, had made a full recovery as his injuries were less severe.

Jason picks up the story. "About two-and-a-half, three months later, I'm still following her son because he's now walking after his fusion, and I'm following her sister who'd had a cervical fracture and healed just fine in a collar and didn't require further surgery."

He received some news about his patient who'd had the seemingly-fatal blood clots.

"I was told she was visiting the Unit, the ICU, and she was in a wheelchair," he recalls. "She had some function. She had some difficulty moving her left arm but she was actually smiling and communicating with people. Everyone remembered her because it had been Mother's Day and her family was so nice and all these different things."

Jason thought of a joke that surgeons sometimes share. "In medicine, we consider the nicer you are, that's your biggest risk factor for survival! Because you can't kill bad weeds!"

This lady was certainly not a 'weed' but had definitely beaten the odds. "About another month or so later, she followed up in my office," says Jason. "She was in a wheelchair and I was scratching my head. I said, 'You are truly a walking miracle.' At that time, she was weaning from her tracheostomy and she started taking a few steps. I saw her again in two months and she was walking. I was completely blown away and I said, 'From a humanist insight, you're not supposed to be alive.'"

He leafed through her charts and remembered that he could have been faulted for taking on what seemed to be hopeless surgery, based on the examination and the CT scans. He looked up at her smiling face. He smiled back at her. "I'm glad I did, obviously," he says.

This is a patient who will never forget Dr. Jason Cormier. Every single Mother's Day, she sends him a long letter and a card.

"I can vouch for this: she's the best cook in the neighborhood and she brings me a nice meal, a special dinner, every Mother's Day," says Jason. "She writes on the Styrofoam container, 'Thanks so much for all you've done and I hope you have a beautiful day.' That means the world to me."

THE SECRET TO SUCCESS?

By Jason Cormier, MD

I WOULD LOVE TO SHARE with you the secret to achieving your goals and being a success at whatever you choose to do. I would love to do that, but the truth is this: there is no secret.

It is important for you to know that I am a very ordinary person. I wasn't born with any remarkable talent. I didn't come from a wealthy family or have anyone who could 'pull strings' for me. I believe that my starting point in Life was no better and no worse than yours.

I had plenty of opportunities to fail and frankly I did, several times, along the way. You will too, and that's okay. You will learn a lot more from things that go wrong than you will from things that go right.

No, there is no secret. However, I can now see that there were certain attitudes that I adopted (and continue to adopt on a daily basis) that have been essential in achieving my goals.

There is absolutely no doubt in my mind that if you adopt these seven attitudes and commit to making them your own, you will win, you will succeed, you will reach your goal. These seven attitudes are not complex or in any way unique. As you read each one, you might say, "I know that." But what you must say is, "I will *do* that." Your success will take a commitment and 'stick-to-itiveness' to stay the course.

Please bear in mind that, whatever your individual goal is, your ultimate goal in life should be achieving a state of happiness, that you are doing your best for yourself and for those around you.

Here are the seven attitudes that I urge you to bring into your own life.

1. It starts with excitement

"Nothing is as important as passion. No matter what you want to do with your life, be passionate." – Jon Bon Jovi

Success in any endeavor has to begin with excitement! What really excites you? What is it that you can see yourself doing that will fill you with joy?

What is it that gives you so much excitement that you forget the time, your headache goes away and you don't even notice the noise of the world around you?

That excitement will come to you, not just from the anticipation of an expected result, but from the actual doing, the journey, the discovery.

When you find that excitement within yourself, you have discovered your passion. The wonderful thing about finding that excitement, discovering your passion, is that you will not only love where that passion takes you but – equally important – you will enjoy all the steps along the way.

In fact, when you are truly excited, the journey becomes the passion. You can't wait to discover the next thing, to perfect the next skill or advance to the next level. If that sounds like the description of playing a video game, in a way it is. That thing that excites you allows you to happily ignore all distractions as you focus on the joy of discovering capabilities you never knew you had!

When you have found that excitement – or when it has found you – it feels completely natural. You're going to want to engage more so there's nothing forced about it. Simply doing it becomes a happy spot for you. It gives you a happy feeling and no matter what, no matter how it turns out, it's always going to have a positive effect because it began in the right space.

For me, music excites me as I create different sounds and beats. I'm finding something that sounds cool or I'm changing something that I think doesn't sound so cool. I don't DJ or create beats because I'm trying to get a paycheck. I do it because it just feels good and I enjoy the moment to moment to moment. I forget that I set out a certain amount of time to deal with it but before you know it, it's four or five hours later and you're still having fun and there's still so much more to do and you still want to do it. That's what excitement does.

Similarly with surgery, it is a passion of mine to be able to change someone's life or give them more time to live. Part of that excitement has always been discovering new and better ways to do what excites me.

Whatever that passion is, it has to be yours, not pushed onto you by someone else. Maybe an older sibling excelled at sports and you feel the expectation that you should do the same, but it just doesn't thrill you the same way.

In another scenario, if your parents built up a successful business, they probably achieved that because it was their passion and they devoted all their energy into it. If you are equally excited about that business and believe you can make it even better, then by all means take the reins and forge ahead. But if your heart isn't in it, if it doesn't excite you, that business could easily stagnate and even collapse. You can't inherit someone else's passion.

When you realize what excites you, that's your passion. It feels like an energy infusion. Things that excite you are going to just keep you pushing and pushing, almost like a "runner's high" that takes you to a place of happiness and achievement.

I've heard it said that winners in the race forget they're in a race; they just love to run. When you realize what makes you "love to run," you have discovered what excites you. That's your passion. Now follow it!

2. Convert your dreams into goals

"Your goals are the road maps that guide you and show you what is possible for your life." – Les Brown

We all have dreams about what we'd like to do, places we'd like to go, the person we'd like to be. Sadly, for most people, that's all they ever are: dreams.

A dream only becomes reality when we create a plan of action to make it happen. And that all begins with setting a goal. Your goal might be: "I will become a successful trial lawyer," or "I will pitch for a Major League Baseball team," or "I will set up and lead a reading program for underprivileged kids in my town."

Your goal is the end result that you are going to achieve. The achievement of it will be built on a series of steps – or mini-goals – along the way. Those steps form your action plan. When I set my goal of playing professional basketball, my action plan began with practicing every single day. My next step was to improve my skills to beat my next-door neighbor one-on-one, the best player in the neighborhood. When I achieved that, my next mini-goal was to beat the best kid at high school and so on. On my way to pro ball, I made it my goal to convince Coach Dale Brown that I was good enough to play on the hallowed court at LSU.

I had to create the same kind of action plan when I returned to LSU and doctors became my heroes as I worked as a lowly transporter at the hospital in Baton Rouge. To become a surgeon, I knew I would first have to get my grades up to par, then achieve at least a

BSc degree. From there I would have to be accepted at med school, I would have to attain a medical degree and then devote years to additional training to become a surgeon. All of these were steps along the way; individual parts of my action plan that had to be completed before I moved on to the next step and then the ultimate goal.

Write it down! When it's in writing it becomes a physical thing instead of just an idea or a wish. Put your goal in writing and list the steps that you will take to achieve that goal. When you check off each step, you will feel a surge of motivation to move on and conquer the next step. Maybe it is literally in writing, pinned to a wall or stuck on the fridge with a magnet where you'll see it every day. Or maybe it is on your phone or laptop, the first thing you see every morning and the last thing every night.

It can help to share your goals with someone you trust. When I told my friend Dallas, "I'm going to be a neurosurgeon," I had committed myself to the goal and he gave me his full support and encouragement as I progressed. In a way, by telling him my goal, I had made a pledge to him as well as to myself, and he was there for me as I completed each part of my action plan.

A long time ago, I was told that actions define your purpose. That meant a lot to me because you could just be full of words but when you put it into action then it's truly a purpose. I believe that's one of the main pillars of success.

There are positive goals but there are also what I call negative goals and I know that sounds strange. Your positive goal, of course, is what you want to achieve. Your negative goals are determinations of what you don't want to happen in your life. These might be, "I'm not going to be a deadbeat; I'm not going to end up in jail; I'm not going to get pulled into a toxic lifestyle; I'm not going to have a broken family."

I truly believe you have to have those negative goals alongside your positive goals. You have to know the things you don't want to have in your life. Understanding and committing to these negative goals is very important when you're trying to avoid distractions that can nudge you off course.

Whatever your individual goals are, I believe the ultimate goal for all of us is the same: a state of happiness. You want to be happy, you want to be successful, you want to make a difference, you want to have some purpose. You want to have knowledge and know that you have made the right decisions. You want to leave a legacy. Above all, you want serenity, that feeling of calm tranquility that comes from achieving the right kind of goals.

The acquisition of wealth won't bring you that serenity, but the way you use wealth certainly could. For me, the goal was never to get to the pinnacle of basketball which would be the all-star game or the SEC championship. It wasn't getting to the pinnacle of medicine to become a famous surgeon. Along my journey, the checkpoints continue to be: Am I giving back? Am I contributing to the wellbeing of others? Am I always reaching into my reservoir of passion and excitement to deliver 'the best me that I can be?'

As a human being, I know I am sometimes going to fall short in that regard and you will too. But at the same time, as long as you know that's what you're aiming for, I think those are really the true tenets of what goals are all about.

Your goals are uniquely your own, but I believe you must ask yourself: Will achieving this goal, and the journey towards it, bring me to a place of happiness, tranquility and fulfillment?

3. Focus on staying focused

> "You don't get results by focusing on results. You get results by focusing on actions that produce results." – Mike Hawkins, inspirational speaker

Staying focused – on anything – is getting more difficult every day as technology finds new ways to grab our attention. It can feel as if our brains are like castles in a video game, under constant attack by relentless invaders who use every trick in the book to distract us, breach our defenses and get inside our brains. If you remember the story of the Trojan Horse, the really clever invaders simply put the distraction in front of us and we invite it inside!

For years, it seemed every employer would say they were seeking someone who could "multitask" and every resumé would promise that the applicant was a great "multitasker." But recent clinical studies have shown that attempting to multitask is counterproductive and you are actually less effective at each task when you skip back and forth rather than focusing on one at a time. You may convince yourself that you can instantaneously switch between tasks, but however smart you are (or think you are), there is a time lag while your brain has to refocus on the new or revisited task. A Stanford University study concluded that multitasking may take up to 40 percent more time than addressing one task at a time, particularly for complex tasks. See yourself as a 'single tasker'!

To achieve your goal, you must focus on successfully completing each of your mini-goals – those steps along the journey to your overall goal. Complete one step, then move on to the next. You've probably heard the saying attributed to Desmond Tutu, "There is only one way to eat an elephant: a bite at a time." Your eventual goal might seem overwhelming, maybe even unattainable, when you are constantly being pulled in different directions every minute of every day. But focus on taking one bite of the elephant – achieve one mini-goal or even one part of one mini goal – and your brain will reward you with a sense of achievement and satisfaction. Take too big a bite, or too many bites at one time, and you'll choke. You'll give up on the goal.

Think of a time when you set yourself a task and you actually did it successfully. Even something relatively trivial such as washing and vacuuming the car, finishing an essay ahead of schedule or writing a difficult note of sympathy to a friend who lost a loved one. You felt a sense of achievement. That reward that your brain gives you isn't imaginary, it is a real thing: a release of dopamine, known as the "feel good" neurotransmitter.

Compare that to another time when, at the end of the day, you realized you hadn't done that one thing you promised yourself you'd take care of. You got distracted and lost your focus. You probably felt a little frustrated, even annoyed with yourself. One thing is certain: your brain did not reward you with a rush of dopamine!

I can tell you from experience, when you're participating in athletics and you're competing, there are a lot of things thrown at you and it is extremely challenging to get past all that. Looking back, I'm not sure how I survived some of it! But I believe the key was maintaining my focus. As I have said, as a kid I focused on improving my basketball skills one step at a time until they became second nature to me.

Staying focused isn't easy and I found that out the hard way. When I went back to LSU, it became apparent that I had gotten distracted by the trappings of the athletic lifestyle. A turning point for me came when I sat down with Dr. Sam McCluggage and he told me that there was only one way that I would be able to get back on track and achieve my goal of becoming a surgeon.

Listening to him, I realized that my goal was achievable but demanding. The only way to make it a reality was to approach it the way I had approached basketball. I had to focus exclusively on completing each step of my journey.

To use another sports analogy, trainers often outfit thoroughbred racehorses with blinders (sometimes called blinkers) that are cups attached to the horse's bridle or a hood. The blinders reduce the horse's field of vision so he is focused solely on what is directly in front of him, masking out all the distractions crowding in on him. In a steeplechase, the horse can focus on jumping each fence as he goes around the course. I had to be like that racehorse and focus on reaching the Finish Line in every race, jumping one fence at a time.

I will paraphrase what Dr. McCluggage said to me and I will pass these words on to you:

Only you yourself can stop you from achieving your goal. Don't let relationships stop you, don't let romantic entanglements, don't let peer pressure, don't let envious detractors, don't let cynical friends, don't let anything or anyone distract your focus and stop you from achieving your goal.

His words made me realize it's going to be me and the Good Lord. I knew God wasn't going to let me down so if I failed it was going to be on me. Once you understand that, you commit to going where you believe you belong and where you feel a calling. You put it on your own shoulders and you understand that you have faith and it IS going to happen.

4. The power of persistence

"Ambition is the path to success. Persistence is the vehicle you arrive in." – Bill Bradley

Once you set your goals, it's persistence that's going to keep you driving towards that goal, whatever that goal may be. It's fine that you have a calling and have passion in everything you do. But persistence to me is no matter what it takes, if you really want to accomplish that specific goal, you're going to stay at it and stay at it. You're going to put your head down and drive until you're done.

As you have seen, when I was a transporter, I continually called the Nursing Director in the operating room, Genie Woodring, until she found a way for me to work in the O.R. I wasn't going to give up until she said yes. If I hadn't persisted relentlessly, I would never have taken my first step beyond the 'Forbidden Door' of the O.R.

For me, when it came to medicine, I didn't look at how things would be the next day. I looked at where I wanted to be in the next ten or fifteen years. It made doing what I had to do the next day a little bit easier because I was able to keep going, doing what had to be done that day, and it felt less intimidating. Each day felt like a small victory.

Not long ago, I was invited to return to my former high school as part of a program where alumni talk about career opportunities. As I entered my old classroom, I remembered being in that seat when I was a kid. A doctor had come to talk to us, just as I was doing that day. He talked to us about what we would need to do if we wanted to become doctors. Frankly, it was scary! It was nerve-wracking to hear him say, "Well, you're going to have to go to college for four or five years, you've got to go to med school for four years and you have to train for another seven or eight years." I was like, "My goodness! Those are some serious numbers! Who wants to do that!"

Then, when I returned to the high school and stood in front of the class, I remembered that, after the doctor had spoken to us, the school recorded an interview with each student. They asked us, "What do you want to do with your life? Where do you see yourself in ten years?" My mom had kept the recording of my interview and when I watched it years later, I saw myself saying, "I want to be a doctor!" I could see myself becoming a doctor, doing rounds and so on. I watched it and I was like, "Oh my gosh! What was I thinking!"

I would remember that day a few years later when I resolved to become a surgeon. That doctor's talk and the taped interview made me realize that ten years of training is a long time, but if I don't do it, in ten years I'll still be ten years older, I just won't be a doctor.

I could see that if I didn't do anything with my life, that was going to be unsatisfying and could become quite expensive. Certainly, just 'being cool' becomes quite expensive! But if I put my head down and I struggle through it, if I do whatever I can to attain that goal, I can make it work. It helped when I understood that I'm not the only one that's going to have to go through that. There are a number of people that will be going through it too, so I know it's something that's doable, it's something that I can accomplish. But I have to keep going and I have to believe in myself.

I have to give my mother credit because as a single mom raising four kids on a teacher's salary, her persistence drove her to provide for us so that we could have food on the table and clothes on our backs. She got us through a private school on her own back. We had work scholarships and grants we had to do for school, but at the same time, she worked hard every day with the goal of seeing her children succeed in life. She's got calluses on her hands from working extra hours and taking on extra jobs, she's got calluses on her knees from praying for us, and through her persistence, she got us through.

A successful real estate agent once told me about the time she started her career. She joined an office as a complete rookie and had no sales leads. The senior broker assigned a specific neighborhood to her and told her to go door-to-door and ask the owners if they would like to list their home for sale with her. As you can imagine, this seemed like a daunting task because the broker estimated that she would need to talk to around two hundred homeowners before she got her first listing.

It was almost enough to make her quit before she started, but she came up with a way to make it feel less painful. At that time, her commission on the sale of a house in that area would be about $3,000.00. If she needed to make two hundred personal sales calls, that averaged out to $15.00 per call. She started going door-to-door and every time the door was shut in her face, she would say, "Thank you. I've just made $15.00!" Sure enough, she signed her first listing and when the house sold, she received her commission check. Instead of feeling she had been rejected a hundred and ninety-nine times, she saw each call as a small installment on her eventual commission. Since then, she has become very successful and no longer needs to make cold calls, but she still understands that you have to hear "No" a lot of times on the way to hearing a "Yes."

It's hard to imagine it now, but author J. K. Rowling was turned down by at least twelve publishers to whom she submitted her first novel, *Harry Potter and the Sorcerer's Stone*. She was recently divorced from a brief marriage that she described as 'toxic,' she was the single mother of a small child and was living in abject poverty on a small amount of public assistance. She finished writing the book on a typewriter in local cafés with her infant daughter on a chair beside her.

Believing she had written a worthwhile book, she finally convinced an agent to represent her. Together, they sent out submissions and received nothing but rejection slips from every publisher. Eventually, one publisher brought home a sample chapter – unread – and his eight-year-old daughter picked it up. An hour later, she ran down from her bedroom and excitedly asked her father for the next chapter because she had to find out what happened. Realizing there could be a market for the book, the publisher signed Rowling to a publishing contract. The Harry Potter books have sold more than 500 million copies and have been turned into a series of hugely successful movies.

Later, Rowling would say that she had hit absolute rock bottom when she was writing that first book. "I was set free because my greatest fear had been realized and I was still alive," she said during a speech at Harvard. "And I still had a daughter, whom I adored, and an old typewriter and a big idea. And so rock bottom became the solid foundation on which I rebuilt my life."

With her eyes locked onto the goal of publishing a book and making a living while doing what she loved, Rowling refused to give up. To her, each rejection was another part of that foundation and she just kept on going.

The motivational speaker Jim Rohn has said, "Motivation is what gets you started. Habit is what keeps you going."

There is really no alternative to sticking to it and driving forward one day at a time. The way to maintain your persistence is to turn your actions into a habit. For that rookie real estate agent, the habit that led to her success was knocking on doors. In my case, it was practicing every evening at the basketball net in our driveway. Then, with my sights on a medical career, it was the daily habit of acquiring the next piece of knowledge or improving a necessary skill.

When any action becomes a habit, you don't think about doing it, you just do it.

Whether we admit it or not we all have habits, but they are probably bad habits. Maybe it's coming home, slumping on the sofa and immediately turning on the TV. It isn't something you think about, you just do it. It's a habit.

When you find the thing that excites you, that ignites a burning passion inside you and you've made it your goal to achieve it, make it a habit to take the actions that will take you there, step by step. Each step you complete will be your small victory, another brick in the foundation that the achievement of your goal is built upon.

5. See challenges, not obstacles

"Obstacles don't have to stop you. If you run into a wall, don't turn around and give up. Figure out how to climb it, go through it, or work around it." – Michael Jordan

To put it simply, obstacles are bad, challenges are good.

An obstacle blocks your way; it's a barrier that prevents you moving forward. However, a challenge is a stimulating exercise; something that needs your physical or mental effort in order to be done successfully. In other words, a challenge – unlike an obstacle – is a problem that can be solved, even if you cannot immediately see the solution.

When a teacher gives her students a set of math problems, her objective isn't to block their progress or impede their education. The objective is for the students to solve the problems; to show they understood the lesson prior to the test and they are developing their problem-solving skills.

Your life, like mine and everybody else's, will inevitably confront you with problems. The way you see those problems determines if they will be obstacles for you or challenges. As a simple example, you are setting out on a road trip and come across a traffic tailback because of emergency road repairs. The vehicles ahead of you are at a dead stop. Another driver sees that as an obstacle, the trip is ruined; might as well just give up and go home. But you simply see it as a challenge and you find a detour around the blockage and continue your journey. It might mean resetting the GPS, checking a road map or simply applying some common sense. Sure, it might take a little more time and a bit more effort than you originally planned, but you saw it as a challenge and arrived at your destination. But the other driver gave up, convinced that it wasn't worth trying.

Yes, that's an example of a minor problem but it demonstrates your attitude to it. A more serious example could be two patients who both receive a diagnosis for the same illness. The first patient sees the diagnosis as devastating; an immovable obstacle to all their hopes and dreams. The second patient is understandably shocked and dismayed but can soon see it as a challenge, discussing options with medical staff and working on a treatment plan.

Reps from medical device manufacturers are frequently in the O.R. with me during a procedure because they are intimately familiar with the specific device and the accompanying toolkit I will be using. I recall a day in the O.R. during a complex surgery when a spine rep said, "Looks like you're having a bad day."

I replied, "My definition of a bad day in the O.R. is when somebody dies. I can't have bad days. I have challenging days."

Challenging days present problems that you have to overcome. You have to have a plan B, a Plan C, a Plan D. There IS a way around the problem. Ideally you know the way; if not, you have to find it. That's the challenge.

Sometimes in the O.R., I look up at the spine reps when we're struggling with the instrumentation and I say, "We will win this game. Some kind of way, we're going to win. We have to win because the patient is counting on us."

That's how I drive through each procedure. That's how I drive through different things in my life. One way or another, I'm going to win this game. I'm going to win it. I'm going to trust my belief system. I've already said my prayers. I have my belief and I know God is on my side and I'm going to win whatever or however that win is.

As you can see, this is positive self-talk. It has become a habit for me to use positive self-talk. You can think of self-talk as an internal dialogue that is constantly occurring, influenced by your subconscious mind. To succeed at any endeavor, it is essential to replace your negative self-talk with positive self-talk.

The words you use in your internal dialogue have the power to build you up or tear you down. When your internal voice is saying, "There's no way I can ever find a solution," you are convincing yourself that you are being blocked by some obstacle beyond your control. You're giving yourself an excuse for failure. But when you throw the switch and turn the negative into positive self-talk, you tell yourself, "I will do everything I can and I will make it work."

I have proved to myself that when I frame any situation in a positive internal dialogue, it takes on the form of a challenge rather than a barrier. I am already mentally wording it in terms of how I'm going to solve the problem. I encourage you to catch yourself when you feel negative self-talk forming in your mind. Mentally re-word the situation in terms that your subconscious accepts as doable, fixable, solvable.

Tell yourself that you will give it your all; you will bring it to the table and you will leave a winner. It doesn't matter what the scoreboard says. At the end of the day, you saw the opportunity and you accepted the challenge and you won because you put your heart and soul into it. That's the win, not the score on the scoreboard. It's how much you put into it.

6. *Education unlocks doors*

*"Education is a progressive discovery of our own igno-
rance."* – Will Durant

When we think of education, we naturally think of school and
college. For my siblings and me, the importance of education was
something we heard about every day from our mother, and we
probably rolled our eyes and gave each other knowing glances
when she said it.

At high school and then at LSU, mom reminded me – and my
coaches – that I was there to get an education, not just play basketball. As you have read here, my mother and I have had our
differences. However, I realize that as a teacher, she saw firsthand
the benefits of getting an education and, perhaps more importantly, the lifelong disadvantages of not getting one.

Of course, I couldn't have become a neurosurgeon without the
very specific education I received at medical school, and I
couldn't have gotten to medical school if I hadn't received a high
school diploma and then college degrees. As I've said, those were
steps along the way to achieving my goal.

However, I want you to see education as more than a framed
diploma, proud parents and something to put on your resumé
when you are looking for a job.

I believe it is important for you to think of education as something that isn't confined to what happens in school. Sitting in a
school classroom while a teacher talks to you or sitting in a college study hall while a professor delivers a lecture isn't education.
It's just somewhere to sit.

The actual education takes place inside you. The classroom
may be where education is delivered from, but it is inside your
brain, your heart and your soul where the education actually

happens as you absorb it – or doesn't happen if you reject it.

Essentially, all education is self-education.

Education can take place on the basketball court, on the football field and at any sport that you participate in. You probably don't think of it as education, but that's what it is. You are not only learning the basics of the sport and how to excel at it, you are learning skills and attitudes that will stay with you for the rest of your life.

Education takes place at home, too, as you learn how to interact with siblings and other family members; essentially another facet to teamwork.

When you add that all together with the classroom education you receive in school, you can see the one thing they all have in common is the quote by the American author and philosopher Will Durant that appears at the top of this section. In fact, the entire quote is this: "Sixty years ago I knew everything; now I know nothing. Education is a progressive discovery of our own ignorance."

To me, that embodies everything about what education really is. Every day, we discover something we didn't know before. Life is a voyage of discovery and the older we get the more we realize how little we know. As you journey towards your goal – that thing that excites and motivates you – you will eagerly seek out the knowledge and experience that draws you ever closer to achieving it. But when you get there, you might be surprised at how much more you discovered along the way that wasn't directly connected to your goal. You've acquired an education.

You will find that education goes far beyond what you learn in school. In fact, many of the people that we think of as the most successful didn't really have a traditional, well-organized education.

One example is Thomas Edison. He had very little formal education as a child and only attended school for a brief period. He probably had learning disabilities that we would now describe as dyslexia and ADHD and he had developed a hearing impairment at around the age of twelve. As a result, his schoolmaster told Mrs. Edison that Thomas was "addled." His furious mother told the teacher that he didn't know what he was talking about and that her son had more brains than the teacher did. She took Thomas out of school and homeschooled him herself until he was sixteen.

He later said that he was always a curious child and taught himself a great deal because of his fascination with how things worked and how to make them work better. It became his passion and he once told an interviewer, "I never did a day's work in my life. It was all fun."

Edison went on to be recognized as one of the world's greatest inventors with more than 2,300 patents worldwide with inventions that continue to be part of our lives today, including a battery that would power an electric car.

Edison was not alone in being labeled as having learning disabilities. Albert Einstein probably suffered from a type of autism or Asperger's Syndrome and was often in trouble for not paying attention in class. Louis Pasteur was diagnosed with both dyslexia and dysgraphia – difficulty in reading and writing – but still developed vaccines for anthrax and rabies. He also discovered the process named after him, pasteurization, that kills bacteria in milk. Being different does not disqualify you from achieving success.

When I decided on a medical career, I vowed to become the world's greatest thief! I watched my mentors. I observed what they did, I closely studied their techniques and I saw what made them so good at what they did. I 'stole' what I saw them do and how they did it. I was able to incorporate what they did into my own skill set until I was as good as they were, with the goal of being even better.

I did the same with basketball, endlessly studying tapes to learn the small differences that made the excellent players stand out from the merely good players. I then did my best to adapt what I learned into my own game.

I encourage you to do the same as you follow your passion: be a thief! Find people who are doing what you want to do; study how they do it; learn from them and put your own spin on it.

Of course, when you are this kind of thief, you are not stealing anything that someone else has created and then claiming that it is yours! You are simply watching them, listening to them, learning from them. You are making mental notes and absorbing their knowledge. The French movie director Jean-Luc Godard, who openly admitted building on what he'd learned from the work of directors who had gone before him, said, "It's not where you take things from, it's where you take them to."

You're educating yourself as to what you need to do. Are you going to learn this to where you can replicate it and improve upon it? It works the same from the simplest to the most complex activity. Your education is your ability to learn, challenge your own ignorance and put yourself in a situation where you want to be successful at whatever it is you do.

Each thing that you do, whether you're cleaning the glass or rebuilding somebody's spine, you want to make your mark, you want to leave your footprint, if you will, on whatever it is you touch, and you can only do that by working hard in preparation. That is your education.

In sports, before a game you need to educate yourself as to what the opposing team is going to do and what you're going to do, in each possible situation that might occur. That's the so-called pre-game. In any sport, there's always preparation, and that preparation to me, is the state of educating yourself. It's a state of training yourself. It's a state of learning what you need to know to prepare yourself for whatever activity you're about to engage in.

I believe that ignorance is nothing to be ashamed of. It simply means there is something you don't understand or something you don't know enough about... yet! The shame comes when you refuse to accept that you don't understand it and choose not to learn.

When you lock in on your passion and it becomes your goal to achieve it, you will happily dive into the education that you'll need to get there. And when you do, like Edison, you'll say, "It was all fun!"

7. Finding inspiration and inspiring others

"The purpose of life is to discover your gift; the work of life
is to develop it; and the meaning of life is to give your gift
away." — David Viscott.

Inspiration can come to you when you least expect it.

Inspiration has to start within your own belief system, whatever that is for you. For me it's God. However, inspiration is all around you, when you are open to it.

I'm inspired by my significant other and the challenges and struggles that she has undergone and the struggles that we go through together. She makes me want to be a better person for her, for me and for everybody else. She is my inspiration each and every day.

For you, it might be a family member or a close friend who is faced by serious challenges but keeps on pushing forward and doing what has to be done for the good of those who rely on him or her.

I believe what often sparks inspiration is what I call 'drive.' When I think about drive, I see it as an unrest or a discomfort within you.

There's tension; you feel there's something missing, almost like someone that's thirsty and that person is going to be driven, to be inspired, to get something to drink to quench that thirst.

There's tension if you're hungry for something missing in your life and you've seen other people that are hungry in the same way. I could see that Dr. Mark Hadley was a hungry person and my high school coach Danny Broussard was too. I could feel the hunger within them to achieve excellence at whatever they do. That kind of hunger is contagious! As a member of their teams – one in an operating room, the other on a basketball court – I was inspired to drive for my own level of excellence.

One challenge can be maintaining that sense of inspiration when you seem to have reached a certain plateau of achievement. How do you stay hungry? Some professional boxers, after they win the belt and attain their millions of dollars, find that they don't feel that hunger anymore. The same thing can happen to musicians and recording artists: after years of struggle, they finally have a No. 1 album but then cannot find the inspiration to push for greater creative success.

Sometimes, competition with someone you admire can be your inspiration. In the late 1960s, The Beatles and The Beach Boys were fans of each other's work and the innovations they created thousands of miles apart – The Beatles in Liverpool, England, and the Beach Boys in California. That inspirational competition arguably led to two of the greatest albums in popular music history, *Pet Sounds* by the Beach Boys in 1966 and *Sgt. Pepper's Lonely Hearts Club Band* by the Beatles in 1967.

My inspiration for creating music is that I want to make people feel good. When I create music that makes other people feel good, it makes me feel good. At times when I'm in a not so pleasant place and I want to go to a place that's happy, I go to music because music does that for me.

You can find inspiration in your social group, the people you surround yourself with. When your peer group consists of people with a positive attitude who are working towards achieving their own goals, their upbeat outlook will inspire you to maintain an optimistic attitude on your own journey.

But if you're surrounded by people that have nothing but excuses as to why they're failing, if they're going to blame it on their gender, their ethnicity, and any number of different things, then I believe that you're set up for failure. People that are miserable are busy being miserable until they find themselves in the midst of other miserable people.

When you surround yourself with positive, successful people, you're going to be too busy being happy and successful to be dragged down to the level of those who are dead set on being miserable.

As you can see, I believe there are two kinds of peer relationships. There is peer pressure where the people around you don't want you to succeed, to move onward and upward. In fact, they want the opposite: they want you 'down there' with them, reinforcing their belief that effort is pointless and failure is inevitable. "Misery loves company" is an apt description for that kind of destructive relationship!

Instead of peer pressure, seek out peer support. That's where you will find your inspiration and the motivation to stay on track and more importantly to feel confident and stay happy. A supportive person is one who might say, "This is how I did it. Let me help you out." It's a person you can trust.

I encourage you to investigate something called the RAM chart that is a guide to how you can look at people or relationships before you commit. RAM is an acronym for Van Epp's Relationship Attachment Model. It consists of a diagram that looks like a stereo equalizer with five sliders that you can move up or down as you evaluate any relationship. It is often used to assess romantic relationships, but I've found that it's equally effective when it comes to friendships and business relations.

I focus on the middle three of the five 'sliders.' The first consideration is, 'Can I trust this person?' Secondly, 'Can I rely on them?' Thirdly, 'Can I commit to them?'

I urge you to think about those things when it comes to who should be in your group of peer support, the friends and associates that you surround yourself with. Those are the people in your social group that will inspire you and in turn you will inspire them.

Dr. Najeeb Thomas told me that he believed that neurosurgery was so awesome because, as a surgeon, you are only as good as your last complication and the way you dealt with it. In the world of entertainment, you are only as good as your last performance. In sport you are only as good as your last game or contest.

See your life in those terms and it will inspire you to be a better person each and every day.

The Seven Essential Attitudes

Keep this summary of your seven essential attitudes where you can see it and be motivated by it every day.

Find Your Excitement
- What excites you?
- That's your passion!
- Vow to follow it
- Follow *your* passion, not someone else's!

Mini-Goals Lead to Big Goals
- An action plan elevates your dream into a goal
- Set a goal that is achievable but challenging
- Set mini-goals that are steps on the journey
- Share your goals with a trusted friend or loved one

Focus on Staying Focused
- Focus on actions that bring results
- Be a single tasker not a multitasker
- Be a racehorse with blinders; jump one fence at a time with your eye on the Finish Line
- Don't let anyone or anything distract you from achieving your goal

Nothing Beats Persistence
- Vow to do something every day that gets you closer to your goal

- Make steps toward your goal a daily habit
- Don't think about doing it; just *do* it
- See rejection as a pointer to your next step
- Never, never, never give up!

See Challenges Not Obstacles
- There are no obstacles in your life, only challenges
- Obstacles give you an excuse to fail
- Challenges give you the motivation to succeed
- Use self-talk to picture challenges not obstacles
- Say, "I don't have bad days, I have challenging days."

Education is a Voyage of Discovery
- A progressive discovery of our own ignorance
- Become a 'knowledge thief'
- Take an expert's knowledge and make it your own
- All education is self-education
- Education is preparation for achieving your goal

Be Inspired, Inspire Others
- Find inspiration in those you love and in those you admire
- Be inspired by people who have a hunger to succeed
- Recognize that hunger within yourself
- Build your social group around positive, upbeat people
- Seek peer support, ignore peer pressure
- You are inspiring others, even if you don't know it

*Dr. Jason Cormier, neurosurgeon, musician and auto racing enthusiast,
in his element at the Kentucky Speedway.*

SINCERE THANKS...

In sincere gratitude and appreciation to everyone who generously shared their thoughts, impressions and memories that became the foundation of this book and its inspiring story, including the following:

Grady J. Abraham
Mohamad A. Allam, MD
James Ambrose
Alan J. Appley, MD
Julian E. Bailes, MD
Bart Bernard
Thomas Bertuccini, MD
Dani S. Bidros, MD
Stanley Blackstone
Andy Blalock, MD
Jeffrey Blount, MD
William Brennan, MD
Danny Broussard
Dale Brown
Marcus Lyle Brown
CJ Bui, MD
M.R. Chambers, MD
John Cobb, MD
Judge Royale Colbert
Luiz Dearaujo, MD
Buffy Domingue
Otis R. Drew, MD
Winfield S. Fisher III, MD
Steve Goldware, MD

Jeff Goodwin
Noah Gordon
Nolan Guidry, Jr.
Angelique Guidy
Mark Gundrum
Mark N. Hadley, MD
Bill Harbin
Mark Harrigan, MD
Mike and Preshias Harris
Mike Hinderlang
Dane and Caprice Huval
Poonie Huval
Keyne Johnson, MD
Patrick Juneau, MD
Janice Kennedy, RN
Armand Ledet
Rick Leoni, MD
Mamerhi Okor, MD
James Markert, MD
Carl 'Groove' Martin
Troy Melancon
Martin Mortazavi, MD
Lyle Mouton
Ilyas Munshi, MD
Shaquille O'Neal, PhD
Jerry Oakes, MD
Mamerhi Okor, MD
Jay Owens
Mel Percy
John Picou
Tony Poirrier
Kaitlyn Poirrier

Patrick Pritchard, MD
Steve Rees, MD
Kristen Riley, MD
John Paul Robertson
Brandon Rochon
Brixton Ruffins
Suzanne Skinner
Matt and CeCe Stuller
Brien K. Syrie
Troy Taylor
Brandon M. Thompson
Jaymie Trahan, MD
Shane Tubbs, PhD
Emmanuel Turner, MD
Robby Waguespack
Dallas Webb
Jay Wellons, MD
Damon Wells
Genie Woodring, RN
and many more

All praise and glory to God for blessing me with family, life, health, opportunities and great people. Thank you for staying by my side, even when my beliefs were challenged to the point of disbelief. Thank you for reminding me that all things are possible through You. Without You, nothing is possible.

To my brother Jeramiah, you are loved and forever missed everyday.

Special thanks to Dr. Jason Cormier's mother Patricia Colbert-Cormier, brother John Cormier and sister Dolores Cormier-Zenon for their unique family memories. I love all of you dearly!

All the hard-working medical personnel at Our Lady of Lourdes Lafayette, Lafayette Surgical Specialty Hospital, and Lafayette General Medical Center.

Much appreciation to Brandon Rochon, many of whose photos in surgery and at the racetrack, add to the understanding of this inspiring true story. We have become brother's for life!

A heartfelt 'thank you' to Shannon Thompson, personal assistant to Jason Cormier, MD, for her boundless help, patience, and positive attitude throughout the creation of this project. Truly you have one of the toughest jobs in the world and you do it extremely well without complaining. Simply can't thank you enough, in addition to James (Shannon's husband) for his support.

To my fiancée Kaitlyn, her dad Tony, our son Brixton, and our daughter Celine, I love you with everything and can't imagine life without each one of you. I have found happiness that I am unable to put in words. You have made me want to be a better man. Through the grace of God, The best decision that I have ever made was to fully open and share my life and heart with you. Thank you for your patience, tolerance and understanding of my crazy life. Thank you for accepting me for who I am and the struggles that I continue to face and overcome.

AFTERWORD

By Dr. Julian Bailes
Renowned neurosurgeon and
Chairman of the Department of
Neurosurgery at the NorthShore
University HealthSystem

JASON CORMIER has been a standout his whole life.

Although he started under austere circumstances, he outworked, out-dreamed and outperformed his peers. As a gifted athlete, he was an outstanding basketball player in high school and went on to play for LSU and later professionally in Europe. He also developed a passion for motorsports, and became an accomplished driver but equally as important, an innovator for driving safety.

However, his single greatest accomplishment has been attaining a Doctor of Medicine degree, then continuing into the specialty of neurosurgery. This field is widely known as one of the most arduous, demanding and time-consuming surgical specialties. Jason has been widely acclaimed as a master technical neurosurgeon, performing the most challenging and intricate brain operations on tumors, aneurysms, trauma, and other difficult procedures. He is recognized by his peers as not only a great technical surgeon, but also as a compassionate and caring physician.

His story is invaluable for the reader as it not only gives the background, motivation, and journey of a great physician, but also the insight as to his philosophy and driving forces, as depicted in "The

243

Seven Attitudes". Dr Jason Cormier is an American success story, a healthcare hero, and a multi talented individual who has shown what hard work, dedication, intelligence, and determination can do. His story should be an inspiration for all people to delve into for inspiration, motivation, and direction.

9 780578 282558